an
INSISTENCE
on
Life

FOULKETALE PUBLISHING
201 West 89th Street, Suite 7H
New York, NY 10024

First Edition October 2013
Manufactured in the United States of America

DESIGNED AND PRODUCED BY JULIA HILL GIGNOUX, FREEDOMHILLDESIGN.COM
PHOTO "NORTHERN FULMAR IN FLIGHT" BY ELSIE TRASK WHEELER © 2013

ISBN-13: 978-1492745204 / ISBN-10: 1492745200
LCCN: 2013917732

an
INSISTENCE
on
Life

RELEASING FEAR OF DEATH TO FULLY LIVE

JANE HUGHES GIGNOUX

FOULKETALE PUBLISHING
NEW YORK

CONTENTS ⋘

Life consists not in holding good cards,
but in playing those you hold well.
—JOSH BILLINGS

A few years ago, I found myself compelled to pay attention to an inner voice urging me to bring together a number of stories that I had either been part of or heard about over the course of many years. I realized that my inner guidance was the same voice that had, back in the early nineties, directed me to explore different cultural beliefs about life, death and beyond through folktales. That inquiry eventually led to *Some Folk Say: Stories of Life, Death and Beyond*. Yet the full explanation for my strong motivation to produce that book did not emerge until seven months after its publication.

Over a lifetime I have learned that when I am strongly motivated to move in a new direction or take on a project, often the true purpose doesn't become clear until much later. While working on *An Insistence on Life*, I wondered again and again about my immediate response to a friend's description of her reaction upon arriving at her close friend's house to attend her friend's twenty-year-old son's memorial, "[the place] was filled with *life*. There was an *insistence* on that." That remark had resonated with me instantly and profoundly, though at the time I wasn't clear exactly why. During the ensuing months, as I continued to think about it, I came to realize my reaction had to do with the underlying thread that connected all the stories in this collection—stories of people dealing with death in transformative ways.

These narratives, then, are a loose collection that has been growing since my initial Harlem Hospital volunteer days with HIV/AIDS pediatric patients starting in the early eighties, with roots going even further back into my early childhood. They offer a range of perspectives on what actually is involved when exploring the mysteries of life, death and beyond. At the time when these incidents occurred, or when I became aware of them, I thought of each as distinct and separate. Now I appreciate how they are related, part of an entangled web—to borrow a term from physics—I had been accumulating throughout much of my life. In a number of the narratives, I have changed the names and certain details to assure privacy.

Concurrently with collecting these stories, I became aware that a childhood perception, glimpsed when I was five, had stayed with me and had been a principal motivation, not just for this project but also for the numerous different initiatives that have captured my attention since the late seventies. For my first eleven years, I lived within the Close of the Cathedral of St. John the Divine on the Upper West Side of Manhattan in New York City. My father, an Episcopal priest, was headmaster of what was then the Cathedral Choir School, a boarding school for young boys, who made up the treble portion of the cathedral's renowned choir of men and boys. Consequently, from a very young age I was exposed to Christianity through the teachings of the Episcopal Church. At some point when I was around five, I remember thinking to myself, "But this can't be the whole story. What about all those people out there on Amsterdam Avenue? They don't know about this good stuff going on in here. The story is that God loves everybody, but what about people who don't know about the God who lives here, inside God's house? It doesn't make sense; there's something missing." Of course, I had no language at that age to express these musings, and who would I have shared them with even if I did? My mother had died when I was four and a half. And there was no way I was going to risk arguing theology with my father. It was forty-five years before I felt safe enough to articulate those long-ago concerns out loud to others.

In the eighties while studying with healers and

personal-growth teachers, quite unexpectedly, I found myself being asked to help women address their mother-daughter relationships. This developed into creating and leading a weekend workshop at a retreat center in Maine. Eight women came bringing their mother-daughter issues, but not their actual mothers. Over the course of two and a half days, they were able to uncover the source of much of what Eckhart Tolle would call their "pain-body." By the end of the weekend, I was feeling spiritually stuffed to the gills, acutely uncomfortable. The women departed, feeling considerably lighter, released from long-held unhappy stories that had defined their relationships with their mothers. They had shed the heavy burdens that had been troubling them, while I, on the other hand, felt as though I was the recipient of their discarded pain.

Once again quite unexpectedly, that evening I attended a healing circle with a group of virtual strangers. The focus was on uncovering wounds of abandonment from the past. For me, I discovered it meant releasing a lifetime of hitherto unacknowledged feelings, brought to the surface during the weekend workshop. Initially, they emerged in the form of uncontrolled sadness, spilling out of my regressed four-year-old self. Supported by the group, my sadness quickly deepened into wrath-filled, primal rage. Uttering fierce guttural sounds, I pounded my fists on a sturdy pillow protecting the designated "mother figure" in the group. At last, totally spent, I collapsed, curled up on the floor, still in my regressed state, but now feeling empty, clear and at peace.

So that is rage, I thought, as I awoke the following morning pondering the events of the night before. All these many years those feelings had lain hidden, unrecognized, unsuspected, but nonetheless present. Now I had a new companion who could analyze events and relationships to help me understand more clearly what was essentially occurring as I made my way through life. Not the sad, feeling-sorry-for–herself four-year-old, and not the rage-filled child either. This internal companion had a very different quality. It was as though I stood apart from myself, centered, witnessing the four-year-old struggle to make sense of what death actually meant and to learn to live without the most central person in her life.

Not surprisingly, also in the early eighties I was drawn to volunteer at Harlem Hospital when I learned there were "boarder babies" there. These were children born at the hospital with HIV or AIDS and with no family involvement. Their mothers, diagnosed with AIDS, had either died at delivery or left the hospital without their babies. Boarder babies lived in the hospital because in those days there was such fear of AIDS that no family dared come forward to claim them and no foster care facilities were prepared to take them. When I first heard about boarder babies, my heart cried out, "Nobody should be abandoned!" Spending time every week with these infants and young children forced me to deal with death—including my personal *relationship* to death—in new ways. Not only did I discover that these children had no fear of death but, I also became aware of the extent to which fear of death motivates so many adults' everyday choices, decisions and behavior. Is this just part of human nature, I wondered, or is it learned behavior?

The Hausa people of West Africa have a simple response to this question in their story, "Life and Death." Here's how the story concludes,

> How can one speak of Death without Life, from which it proceeds? And how can one speak about Life without Death, to which all living things go? Neither can exist without the other.

Over the years, I have included that tale, with its wise conclusion, in many of my workshops.

Those three perceptions—the need for a different story to explain the nature of reality, the purpose of life and the limiting consequences of living in fear of death—underlie all my work, including *An Insistence on Life*. There are times when operating from this foundation feels mighty lonely. It felt like a kind of benediction, therefore, when I heard philosopher, author and activist Cornel West state, during the Interdependence Movement event in New York City on September 11, 2011, "Our obsession with the material world and 'success' is based on fear of death." He said it almost as though it were a throwaway line. But inwardly I cheered, "Hurrah! Here's someone who truly gets it!" On the same occasion, the award-winning ethicist, psychologist and early feminist Carol Gilligan said (more than once), "We have been telling ourselves 'false stories' [about the nature of reality and purpose of life]."

Yet Gilligan's insistence on the need to adopt new stories runs straight into the widely held, yet scientifically inaccurate belief, that life is based on unrestricted competition set in a solely dualistic reality, where everything is either good or bad, true or false, right or wrong. *An Insistence on Life* offers anecdotal evidence to support a very different perspective, one that echoes both the interconnectedness of quantum physics and extensive new scientific research indicating that the central impulse of life is the urge to connect (see bestselling author/journalist Lynne McTaggart's 2011 book, *The Bond: Connecting Through the Space Between Us*). This ever-growing body of scientific evidence rests on top of an impressive collection of perennial wisdom found in many indigenous cultures throughout the world.

Yet today's mainstream society continues to insist that life is a competition to be won at all costs, regardless of the consequences. This belief is almost always coupled with dualism: everything has to be either right or wrong, true or false, good or bad. The difficulty is that these beliefs (I like to call them "stories"), along with the behaviors they generate, are no longer valid in the twenty-first century. The need to let go of them along with a number of other deeply ingrained, yet outmoded societal stories challenges us all. Science tells us that our brains are very good at learning new things. We are less adept at *unlearning* deeply ingrained patterns or habits.

It occurs to me that this period in history—the early part of the twenty-first century—has something in common with the era when we humans had to let go of our firmly held belief that Earth was the center of the universe. It wasn't easy, and it took many, many decades, but eventually we accepted the new story that our "home" is one of several planets circling a star we call the sun. Once we gave up insisting on having the central role in the story of the universe, adjusting to newer and ever more astonishing scientific findings in recent centuries has been challenging for some, but generally less painful. Yet still there is a formidable difficulty with releasing our overwhelming fear of death in order to embrace death as our natural birthright. Most people are quite unaware of the extent to which this fear controls and distorts their lives. There are those, however, who are able to question their unexamined beliefs—to unlock the door marked: DANGER—FEAR OF DEATH WITHIN.

The stories that follow are a sampling from a few of these people. By addressing and releasing their fear of death, they were able to demonstrate their insistence on life. *Not* by attempting to control life, but rather by *including* death, life's partner. They point to the wonder-filled truth that is so often lost in today's materialistic society—life and death are inextricably connected to one another. Their dance is never ending, and the melody is pure love. ❧

ONE

Letting Go

You will know
your next step
from this step.
You will never find it
any other way.
Your intellect
does not know it.
You cannot think
God's reality.
You can only
experience it.
—*EMMANUEL'S BOOK*

Countless times since 1998, when I started leading workshops about various aspects of life, death and beyond, I have observed how often people make comments that indicate they consider death a failure, a punishment, a crime, the ultimate disaster to be feared and avoided at all costs. These ways of relating to death can be a source of enormous pain and suffering for both the dying person and his or her loved ones. While I've become accustomed to the many ways people dance around the subject of death, some folks unable to utter the word itself, I've also noticed, something lurks beneath this discomfort—a form of fear—for they are curious and often seek ways to pierce the shield of their reluctance.

I will never forget a six-foot-plus African American fellow who came to my first workshop in the men's section of a federal correctional complex in 1999. He had the build of a linebacker, and he surprised me when—in response to my query to the fifty men present, "What brought you to attend this workshop?"—he asked quietly, "Why am I so afraid of death?" His honesty and courage impressed me at the time and have stayed with me ever since. With absolutely no preamble, he came directly to the very question that so many people are unable to voice.

Another instance of someone being able to probe

unresolved internal territory came during a workshop, "Stories That Heal," held in an entirely different setting: Jackson Hole, Wyoming. As usual, I started with a folktale from *Some Folk Say*, then I asked people what brought them there, recording their responses on a flip chart. This led to more stories, more questions and more conversation. In addition, people wrote their reflections to some of the questions privately. About twenty-five people participated, several of them men of mature years. At the end of the workshop, as I started to gather up my materials, one six-foot-four, impressive-looking fellow in his pristine blue jeans and western cowboy boots strode up to the front of the room. Towering over me, he stopped directly before me and, bending over, silently enveloped me in a powerful, warm embrace. Straightening, he backed off, and we locked in mutually appreciative eye contact. Not a word was spoken during this encounter, but I could sense that he had broken though a critical barrier—something important had been healed, and he was in a state of profound gratitude.

Transformative moments are not uncommon in workshops. One of my teachers in the early eighties used to say, "A workshop is a place where people come, tools are offered and the people do their work." In 2002, the chief psychologist at a federal prison, where I had previously given a couple of workshops, invited me to design a daylong experience for sixty-five inmates in the low security unit. They were all enrolled in a new six-month intensive pre-release program designed to prepare them for their return to society as responsible citizens. As I worked on this assignment, I realized the overall theme for the day needed to be death and rebirth. First they would let go of their old selves, the selves that had led to being convicted of a federal offense (death). Then they would move into the rebirth: Who am I now? What values and behaviors do I want to embrace in my new life? In addition to small group dialogue, sharing stories, journaling and nonverbal exercises, I introduced a couple of Native American rituals. Deceptively simple in form, these ceremonies can have a powerful, even transformative impact on participants. The men engaged attentively and respectfully in all that was offered.

The following day, I returned to the prison to give a different workshop for another group of men. The psychologist warned me when I arrived that some of the fellows from the day before had asked if they might attend this second workshop. As I was setting up for the day, one of the men from the previous day entered the room. I could see he was excited as he approached. "I want to thank you for yesterday!" he blurted out. "I feel *so much* lighter!" Whatever unresolved questions, heavy resentments or fear-laden issues he might have been carrying, it was obvious he had released them.

During a break at another federal prison workshop, a fellow I estimate was in his late fifties or early sixties sought me out to confess, "In all these years I never understood until now that forgiveness isn't about letting the other guy off the hook! It's about *my* letting go of all that crap! I feel so free!" He, too, was euphoric at his discovery. No doubt, there are thousands, perhaps millions of people around the globe and throughout time who have experienced similar awakenings. Given this fellow's situation, I was especially moved by his words, "I feel so free!" ⋘

TWO

The Missing Piece

Death is like taking off a tight shoe.
—*EMMANUEL'S BOOK*

The summer of 2005, on a road trip through parts of France, Alice and her husband, Harold, had dinner one evening at a cabaret in a town in Burgundy. A small band was playing Duke Ellington numbers. Harold, being a lyricist and lifetime devotee of popular music, knew the lyrics to all the numbers and sang along quietly with the music. During a break, the bandleader came over to Alice and Harold's table. When he heard that Harold was a professional lyricist, he invited him to come over and join the band to perform with them. Harold, who had always loved to sing, took up the offer and became the hit of the evening. He belted out the lyrics to whatever song the band played, much to the delight of everyone present. As Alice says simply, "He was terrific!"

The experience awakened in him a long-suppressed dream of creating a cabaret show of his favorite material from musical theater and other American popular songs of the first half of the twentieth century. When Alice and Harold got back to New York, he decided to make that long-held dream come true. Collaborating with a close friend, who was a brilliant record producer, arranger, composer and piano player, they spent months putting together a program of songs, stories and humorous asides. Then Harold and Alice made a list of their many friends, hired a cabaret on 47th Street for an evening, sent out invitations and prepared for Harold's big night. "It was a huge success. The place was packed," Alice remembered. "In addition to our New York friends, people came from Massachusetts, Florida, New Mexico and California. Everyone loved it!"

Several months after that triumph, Harold was diagnosed with lung cancer. A decade earlier, Alice had been diagnosed with lung cancer that had metastasized to her brain. After the most up-to-date medical protocols failed to deliver a cure, she had turned to alternative healing sources. Among other treatments, she experienced an intense and rigorous Native American Church ceremony that lasted thirteen hours. Afterward, the "road man" who led the ceremony told her that she had been healed, but it would take a while for her body to catch up. Eighteen months later, after numerous CAT scans, her oncologist—initially highly skeptical of the efficacy of these alternative healing protocols—declared her cancer-free. Given his wife's earlier experience, Harold naturally returned to these same healing circles for similar extended Native American ceremonies and procedures. In addition, a constant stream of friends, many from the music and entertainment world, came to sit with him to support his healing. As Alice recalled, "For months we were hardly ever alone. There was lots of music in our apartment during that period, with Harold singing so many of his favorite songs."

In spite of all these efforts, Harold's condition did not improve. He died in February of 2006. He and Alice had been married for forty-three years, but Alice had to put aside her grieving process to continue making a very ambitious feature documentary that she had been producing and codirecting with Harold. Throughout this period, she continued to be profoundly troubled by one question. Why was *she* able to heal from her cancer while Harold, using similar methods and practices, was not? She could find no satisfactory answer to that enigma, and it continued to trouble her deeply.

In April of 2011, Alice took part in one of my workshops: "Exit Plan: For People Who Love Life." "Near the end, all of a sudden I got a very powerful revelation, a real gestalt shift," she told me later. "At last it all made sense. That joyful cabaret performance Harold had given, inspired by the impromptu dress rehearsal the summer before in Burgundy, was the magnificent finale to his life. He'd manifested his one remaining important dream and was ready to move on." Alice's face fairly glowed as she added, "He was done, quite content to make his exit." When this missing piece to Alice's puzzle fell into place that April evening, it was as though a great weight had lifted from her heart. ❦

THREE

Tackling the Great Mystery

Out beyond ideas of wrongdoing and rightdoing,
there is a field. I'll meet you there.
When the soul lies down in that grass,
the world is too full to talk about.
Ideas, language, even the phrase *each other*
doesn't make any sense.

—RUMI

Over many years of observing how
different people deal with death—their own or that of
a loved one—I continue to wonder why it is that some

in the prime of life will succumb to a catastrophic illness, while others in similar circumstances are able to have what are often called "miraculous" recoveries. This existential mystery remains unsolved, of course, but I wonder whether our relationship to death may possibly play a role, not only in whether we are able to survive a given health challenge but also how we experience the entire process.

A few years ago, two male friends, in their prime middle years—unknown to one another—were each diagnosed with different types of lymphatic cancer. In both cases, the news came unexpectedly. Both men were in stable long-term loving relationships. In one situation, the husband, I'll call Gary, physically robust and a devout Catholic, declared he did not want to make cancer the focus of his life. The couple was told the cancer was slow growing.

Consequently, for several years, Gary and his wife, whom I'll call Eleanor, more or less ignored his cancer, "We lived hand in hand with denial and acceptance," she said. "We decided our love for one another would sustain anything." After several years, Gary's doctors determined his cancer had progressed to the stage where chemotherapy and other medical interventions would be necessary.

"Then we got scared," admitted Eleanor. "The focus became, let's try to fix this. We never talked about death. We felt it was more powerful to talk about living." They both found a kind of excitement in the challenge of believing "500 percent in a cure." They kept telling one another, "Miracles do happen."

After a time, Gary's doctors recommended a bone marrow transplant. Even though his system rebelled after this difficult procedure and his suffering was huge, Gary didn't give up. As his condition deteriorated over the course of many weeks, however, he became depressed when he finally realized he was dying. Eleanor at his hospital bed day and night, by her own admission, continued to live in denial.

"Near the end," she told me, "he said, 'I don't want to do this anymore.'" His family arrived at the hospital to say good-bye. "The last three hours were very peaceful; I found that so comforting. Just our two sons and I were with him at the end. I could feel him leave. He didn't have cancer when he left," Eleanor declared.

Much later she realized, "He chose to move on. But at the time, it felt like I was buried in an avalanche sliding downhill." For many months after Gary's death and funeral, Eleanor was totally exhausted, wrung out from her intense and extended efforts to keep her husband alive. Eventually, she found two spiritual teachers to help her deal with her feelings of rage and abandonment. Three years later, she started making a new life with new friends and new adventures. Perhaps most importantly, as she looks back over the time of Gary's illness, she finds that she continues to learn from the entire experience.

"I'm much more comfortable now with the realization that we each have our own paths and that every step Gary took was part of *his* path. At some level he chose to make the journey that he made." Eleanor also has come to accept that souls never die. "He's right here with me but in a different form. I'm not completely OK with this, mind you, I have a ways to go. But I'm a lot more comfortable with it than I was." Eleanor also knows that she, too, has her own path to create and follow so that she's much more conscious of the choices she's making. When faced with a difficulty, she asks herself, "Does this project feel hard because I'm making it hard?" Following that thread, she declares, "I don't know what will happen, but my next adventure will be what it will be and I'm going to enjoy it!"

The other friend diagnosed with lymphatic cancer, I'll call John, was initially led to believe that he had an abscess around his appendix. A laparoscopy revealed a six-inch tumor. During an emergency operation, the surgeon removed not only the tumor, but also one-third of John's large intestine. A couple of hours after surgery, this same doctor called on the hospital house phone to say the biopsy had revealed the tumor was cancerous. Then two hours after that he called again to say it was an especially aggressive type of cancer, and they were transferring him to Mass General because they couldn't handle it there. "They'll probably want to start chemo right away because your cancer is so fast growing, but your chances of survival are small. Chemo reduces the immune system, so most likely, since you won't have had a chance to recover from surgery, infections will take over. Be prepared to leave for Mass General in two hours."

Massachusetts General Hospital is a 200-year-old premier teaching and research hospital in Boston, Massachusetts, affiliated with Harvard Medical School and is well known in medical circles throughout the world. Before his two-and-a-half-hour ambulance ride, John was given morphine and antianxiety drugs so that much of the trip was a blur. Three years later, John told me, "When I first got the word that I was headed to Mass General, I thought this was a death sentence and the cancer had spread throughout my body."

Because he had been heavily sedated, John has no memory of his arrival in Boston or his transfer from the ambulance. He does remember becoming aware of being under a strong light and, when he opened his eyes, seeing six seriously intense interns staring down at him as he lay in an examining room. "How many nuts and bolts will it take to fix this?" John heard these words issuing unbidden from his mouth, quickly followed by the interns' grim expressions transforming as they cracked up with laughter.

Shortly thereafter, John met his new Mass General oncologist. He was a young doctor with a very different perspective on John's condition from his previous specialist back home. This doctor calmly said that his form of lymphatic cancer, while certainly aggressive, was very curable and that in John's case it hadn't spread widely. "You can stay here for a week and then go home for a few weeks to recover before returning to start treatments." He recommended five days of chemo every three weeks for several months.

John had been in AA for twenty years and a follower of Buddhism for slightly longer. He claims that both those spiritual disciplines were important in sustaining him throughout this medical crisis. Thanks to the Mass General chaplaincy program, a Buddhist came to see him from time to time during his hospital stays, and in addition, through the AA support network, occasionally meetings were held in his hospital room. Using the teachings of AA, he continually dealt with his feelings as they arose moment to moment, day to day. In addition, he practiced the "long breath," which his Buddhist teacher taught him by phone from California while he lay in his hospital bed. "The 'long breath' was for me to use while I was having my spinal tap, to take my attention away from the spot where they were puncturing and to preoccupy me with controlling my breath." John found that this and other techniques not only helped him to stay focused and calm himself but also allowed him to keep his partner, Tom, from becoming overanxious. "Throughout it all, Tom's well-being was my main concern."

As soon as he could get his hands on a computer, John sent out an e-mail from Mass General to friends far and near, alerting us to his situation and asking for our support. One of these friends, who like John is partly Native American, was about to leave for a week-long Sioux healing ceremony in South Dakota, when he received John's e-mail. This fellow proceeded to ask all those at the Sioux ceremony to include John in their extended and intense healing rituals and dances.

"I was surprised at how calmly I handled the whole thing," John told me several years later. "I thought if I were going to die, I was in pretty good shape spiritually and didn't have much unfinished business or regret."

Another unexpected form of support came one day when he was back home between his chemo treatments. A friend called to suggest John should go check out some Tibetan monks who were creating a sand mandala for healing at the local museum. John dropped everything and hurried to the museum to watch them work. Once the gorgeous, intricate patterns were completed, he continued to watch as the monks scooped up the brightly colored sand into small bags and offered them to anyone who wanted one. John took a bag and then joined the monks as they marched—in their distinctive saffron-colored robes— down the main street, horns blowing and drums sounding. The local population, mostly unfamiliar with Buddhist ways, stopped in their tracks and watched in astonishment, never before having witnessed such a procession. For John, an experienced Buddhist practitioner, their ceremony was a most serendipitous and welcome gift. When they reached the river, the monks tossed the remaining sand into the stream—returning it to nature—as their final gesture of healing.

Because his cancer was such an aggressive type, his oncologist had John continue to return to Mass General at three-month intervals for a year. This was in addition to the initial five months of intensive chemotherapy and spinal tap treatments every three weeks. Throughout, his Mass General doctor continued to reassure John that he was confident the cancer was gone. These periodic checkups were important, however, to be absolutely sure no cancer cells returned. Eventually, John's hospital visits were reduced to every six months. After three years, John was officially declared cancer-free.

Thinking back over that entire episode, John reflected, "Now that I have been given a second life, I more fully realize how delicate life actually is." He continues to be deeply grateful for both his Buddhist practice and his twelve-step discipline. He feels that both helped him enormously in being able to stay focused in the present, avoiding anxiety-breeding traps of a fear-infested future. "It was all about constantly asking, 'What's *real* here right now and how am I going to deal with it in this moment?'"

What's real? John's question is surely the key one to be asking whenever we're faced with uncertainty. These two situations—tales of different life-threatening cancers—remind me of how I often started my workshop "Embracing Life, Death and Beyond," when I began giving it in 1999.

I would open by offering two very different perspectives on death. One came from the D. H. Lawrence poem, "All Soul's Day."

Be careful then, and be gentle about death.
For it is hard to die, it is difficult to go
through the door, even when it opens.

By way of contrast, I then offered a comment attributed to Peter Pan, "To die will be an awfully big adventure." I invited those present to keep *both* of these ideas in their awareness as we explored together our questions surrounding the great enigmatic mysteries of life, death and beyond. In my workshops, we use folktales and wisdom stories from around the world and throughout time to reflect on the different ways people have come to understand and even appreciate death and its relationship to life. My motivation stems from the recognition of how deeply an ever-present fear of death—often at least partially unconscious—affects people's ability to fully engage with life. This is often accompanied by the awareness that our stories—the meanings we make to explain our life events—are what constitute our life experience. While we can't change the events once they have occurred, we *can* change the story we tell ourselves and others about those events. As I often say during these workshops, life's essentially a matter of storytelling.

This probing into recognizing that we have choices about how we interpret our lives is another step to healing—or making ourselves whole. Many times one hears someone say, "I was upset at the time, but I came to see that what happened was in fact a blessing" or "I was so angry then, but now it all makes sense."

The question is, how do the two stories about people dealing with cancer contribute to the inquiry into our relationship with death that people have explored so many times in workshops? They lead me to wonder about the role fear might have played in these two situations. John, with Tom's help, actively addressed—

one might even say embraced—his fears as they arose. For Gary and Eleanor, their fears, during much of Gary's illness, remained unnamed and largely unexamined. There is no way to assess whether these different relationships to fear influenced the outcome of the two men's cancers. I wonder, could it be possible that Eleanor's distress levels and suffering before and after Gary's death may have been exacerbated by her self-proclaimed overriding fear of death? That question has no answer, of course, but it leads to another question, triggered by Eleanor's awakening to the possibility that each individual is on his or her own journey and ultimately chooses the events of that life. Is that how it really is? Sometimes this is a tough concept to embrace, especially when it concerns life and death, but it surely relieves us of the temptation to cast judgments. ⟪

FOUR

Embracing Life, Death and Beyond

The act of dying is also one of the acts of life.

—MARCUS AURELIUS

A person's relationship to death can greatly influence not just that individual but also an entire community.

Wendy and I were theater majors in the grand and glorious days of Hallie Flanigan Davis's reign at Smith.

I can still see Wendy striding along the path down to "Studes,"—the old theater department building—hair flying, an impish smile on her face, crescent wrench (required equipment for all theater majors) swinging from her blue jeans.

We both took Hallie's playwriting class and teamed up to write the form of play developed in the thirties by the Federal Theatre Project under Hallie's direction—a "Living Newspaper." Our living newspaper was titled *Marijuana*. The department produced it in the spring of our senior year. During our writing sessions, Wendy would pile chairs on top of the seminar room table in the basement of Studes, and then climb up precariously to recline, eyes to the ceiling, spouting dialogue, as I took notes and made suggestions from a safe distance.

After college, Wendy survived a couple of devastating blows during her life. Driving to Mexico with a friend to paint for the winter, the car overturned and Wendy was thrown out onto the desert, sustaining multiple severe injuries. Her full recovery took several years.

She met and married Chuck Gordon, a commercial airline pilot. They had a daughter, Winkie, and they moved to Hong Kong where Chuck flew the rest and recuperation circuit, transporting U.S. military serving in Vietnam to and from designated places, such as Australia and Hawaii, for two-week breaks from combat. After the war ended, they settled in Bermuda where

Wendy became fascinated by flowers and horticulture. Soon after her second child, Davy, was born, it became apparent that he had serious neurological developmental problems. Quite soon after this diagnosis, Chuck left the marriage, and Wendy was utterly devastated.

Eventually her spirits returned, and she gathered up her little family and resettled in Storrs, Connecticut. I helped her move into her first apartment there, where she studied horticulture at the University of Connecticut and made friends in the community. I would visit occasionally, noticing the ever-increasing clutter that surrounded her. Wendy was never one for keeping house; it simply didn't interest her. She seemed oblivious to living in a chaotic jumble. Her charm and appeal came from her vivid imagination that could conjure up delightful flights of fancy. The more practical, grounded aspects of life escaped her—perhaps those very qualities were what drew me to her so strongly. She definitely was a rare bird.

The summer I heard that Wendy had cancer, I called her right away and drove over to Storrs from Rhode Island where I was visiting to have lunch. We had a wonderful day together and laughed a lot. We didn't discuss how she was planning to deal with her cancer or what sort of treatments she intended to pursue. The diagnosis was far too new for her to have fully digested its implications. The visit was simply about two old friends sharing our deep appreciation and love for one another. Bernie Segal's *Love, Medicine and Miracles* sat atop the clutter on her dining-room table, a gift from a friend. I left sensing she would not be following Segal's protocol—taking heroic, alternative measures to heal her cancer.

During the ensuing weeks and months, we stayed in touch by phone. The last time I spoke with her was Christmas 1987. The old Wendy and her familiar optimism were right there, "We're just fine, Janey. We're all here together, we're fine."

A few weeks later when family and friends showed up for her funeral, I discovered that Wendy had been right—everything *was just fine*. Wendy had taken charge of her dying in a way few people can manage. She stayed at home with her children, now grown, connected with the local hospice, saw friends who came to visit regularly. And she had planned her funeral, down to the last hymn.

The organ played the first notes of "Ye Watchers and Ye Holy Ones." One of Wendy's cousins, Cecil, also a college classmate and sister theater major, leaned forward from the other end of the long pew, and we exchanged wicked smiles. Wendy had always said she was jealous because Cecil and I had gone to a high school where we got to sing that gorgeous rousing hymn with all its "alleluias" at our graduation, while her school didn't have anything so grand. Now at last, Wendy could graduate to "Ye Watchers."

We sang our hearts out that morning and listened in awe as Winkie, the minister and friends all spoke of what a gift Wendy had left them in the way she had embraced her dying. At the reception afterward, it was apparent that everyone in that community had been deeply affected, uplifted and healed. As Shakespeare wrote (changing only the gender), "Nothing in her life became her like the leaving it, she died as one who had been studied in her death."

Perhaps Wendy's story relates to the question Peggy Holman asks in her book, *Engaging Emergence: Turning Chaos into Opportunity,* "How do we make space for the whole story—good, bad and indifferent?" In many ways during her lifetime, Wendy had a tough time making space for some of the parts of her story as they unfolded. She sometimes resorted to denial when circumstances overwhelmed her. That's why it was especially poignant that she wholeheartedly embraced her situation when cancer entered the picture. Because she chose to accept this reality, it allowed her family and the entire community to join her and reap the benefits.

Over the years I have often wondered what it was that gave my friend the strength and courage to engage with her dying as she did. She took charge of the final chapter of her life with an energy and clarity that had not always been present during earlier challenges. When her husband left the marriage, I was told she took to her bed for many days, unable to deal with his departure. What everyone recognized when we gathered for her funeral was what a gift her active involvement in this final chapter of her life had been to family, friends and the community. I don't mean to imply that we were exempt from the grieving process, far from it. I still miss Wendy today when I think of her. I wouldn't be surprised if many of her family and friends feel the same. Along with that sense of loss, however, was something important to celebrate that, in a curious way, overrode the grief. How could anyone resist the joyful commitment and triumph she communicated through her attitude and actions? She was determined to walk through this portal with her head held high, just as she used to stride around campus during our long-ago carefree college days. ⚜

FIVE

Standing on the Shore

I am standing on the seashore. A ship at my side spreads her white sails to the morning breeze and steers for the blue ocean. She is an object of beauty and strength. I stand and watch her until at length she is only a ribbon of white cloud just where the sea and sky come to mingle with each other.

"There! She's gone!"

But someone at my side says, "Gone where?"

"From our sight, that's all."

She is just as large in mast and hull and spar as she was when she left our side; and just as able to bear her load of living freight to the place of destination. Her diminished size is in us, not in her.

Just at the moment when you say "There! She's gone!" other voices are ready to go take up a glad shout:

"There she comes!" and that is what we call dying.

—HENRY VAN DYKE, "I AM STANDING ON THE SEASHORE"

I had first met Martha in the mid eighties during a weekend workshop given by Meredith Lady Young, author of *Agartha: A Journey to the Stars*, a book we had both read. It was one of the "channeled" books of that era about the author's extended experiences of receiving direct guidance from a spiritual being she called Mentor. I was fairly new to this sort of phenomenon and eager to learn more about life in the nonmaterial realms. When I struck up a conversation with Martha and discovered she was a psychologist, it surprised me that she, with her training and credentials, was also interested in learning about the very nontraditional experiences of the presenter. As I came to know Martha over the years, I discovered she was always on the lookout for new ways to explore the psyche, learning new techniques to help her clients probe into their interior worlds. Her manner and presence were gentle and mild, concealing her fearless exploratory curiosity and nature.

In the latter part of 2008, Martha wrote an e-mail letter to her large circle of friends and associates advising us, "This may well turn out to be a farewell letter as it looks like I'm getting close to the end of my journey with [lung] cancer." She went on to share some of the details of her situation and that she was now receiving daily hospice care. In describing her current state, she wrote, "I am feeling increasingly tired and weak, with my thoughts turning more toward 'going home' at this point rather than attempting to prolong life in a compromised and painful body. I tried hard for a long time to turn this around with both alternative and conventional therapies. A part of me really wanted to be here to participate in the Great Shift taking place on our dear planet."

Later in the letter she confessed, "I am actually quite looking forward to the Great Liberation. From what I can intuit and have read, it seems that evolution and service continue on the other side, perhaps in even more powerful ways. And it will be such joy to have the veils of limited body consciousness lifted as we return to our home in Spirit."

Martha concluded, "Of course we don't know what lies ahead, but I trust it is something to look forward to where we will build upon our efforts here."

A couple of weeks after Martha's "good-bye" letter, in late November, about fifteen of us received another e-mail from her that began, "We are organizing a prayer vigil team to support my transition to the spiritual realms." She invited us to be part of this vigil team, which met for the first time a few weeks later. When we gathered at Martha's place, most of us expected to find her in bed. Not at all, she was up, dressed and, though quite frail, sat with us in a circle in her living room. In addition to this initial gathering, the vigil group met at least twice more during the next two months. Here are a few excerpts from e-mail exchanges between participants in those circle gatherings.

Yesterday's gathering of twelve of us physically, and the rest of you energetically, was a profound and joyous experience for me and I believe for you as well. I spoke with Martha who was, as always, warm and eloquent in her appreciation for all of us who love her so deeply and are creating a sacred circle to support her passage, as someone said, "to her new cosmic address!"

o o o

I haven't seen her so energized in many months. I felt an atmospheric shift in the room and, sitting next to Martha, a shift in her. Martha appeared to become more buoyant, more luminescent. Maybe the loving reflections and poignant sighs that were *breathed* into the room bathed and lifted her lungs?

o o o

I sense we have been reminding ourselves within Martha's prayer vigil that there are no distinctions within our *oneness . . . No real* boundaries. Neither life nor death can keep us apart from the pure experience of the *one love* of our *creator—our true self—* that is not bound by our earthly conditioning and moorings. *LOVE morphs EVERYTHING!!*

∘ ∘ ∘

I am so grateful for our gathering the other day. Thursday night was the best sleep I've had in years. Sustained, a nurturing, healing sleep, I was held in the energy.

∘ ∘ ∘

My experiences in the "Martha" group are bringing more clarity by the day to my existence. There is a feeling of trust at a higher level in that group than I have experienced in any kind of group work before. Because of the nature of the group, and the offerings there, it is very noticeable to me that I seem to be walking in more awareness all day, every day.

∘ ∘ ∘

Martha, I love your fearlessness . . . I am awestruck by your heightened energy and the courage it must take to bring us all along on this *revelation ride.*

In response, Martha wrote us after our first vigil gathering,

> I can't begin to tell you how much it means to me that you have chosen to add your energy to support my transition in this way. My experience in the group on Wednesday was truly extraordinary. I felt so touched and held by your love and the love from the subtle realms. That was very tangible for me as well. I was in ecstasy all night.
>
> You have given me such a precious gift. I'm still trying to fully receive it. As I mentioned, I hesitated at first to ask people to give of their time in this way. 'People are busy with their own lives. They must have more important things to do.' Yet I was called to reach out and imagine my surprise when people came back saying they were honored to be asked.
>
> Since then the moments of breakthrough to the consciousness of the next realm have become more frequent. It's about Love and Oneness, about being part of one another at a very profound level. I know that you will help to bring forth the greater opportunity and meaning of this transition and make this a true celebration. I am honored by your participation and rejoice in it.

During the course of our vigil gatherings, Martha told us that even though at one level she felt ready to make her transition, a part of her was still resisting fiercely because there was still work she wanted to complete. Ever the innovator and consummate professional, she admitted that the resister part of her felt fearful and not ready to let go. When I asked Martha if she would allow me to use pieces of her reflections to the group in some writing I was doing, she replied most generously that she would be honored.

Two months after we first met, one of the conveners of our group wrote, "Martha is in bed and entering her last phase. She is well cared for by the team of nurses, aides and a lovely hospice volunteer. Her heart is full of love and gratitude, and she especially wanted me to convey to each and every one of you her profound appreciation for all you have done for and meant to her."

A week later we received another e-mail. "Our Martha peacefully took flight at 2:20 this morning. This occurred just hours after seven of us had sung a beautiful gospel song to her that Catherine [her daughter], through yet another synchronistic happenstance, had received. Martha's favorite number was seven, and here we are on the seventh day of April!"

After a joy-filled funeral well attended by a large number of Martha's friends, the vigil group felt a need to meet once more to share some of the powerful thoughts and feelings that were stirring within us. This time we met at my place and Catherine joined us. One person's comments after this session capture the group essence.

> I found the whole experience to be incredibly intimate and profoundly sacred. The energy in the circle when we had our vigil group was full of life and density. I sensed a connection to heaven and earth and felt as though we were joined there by other energies/spirits. I felt a proud peace and silence when we were together.
>
> What was also striking was the openness and honesty of the whole process. The circle of giving and receiving was strongly in play. It was beautiful. It felt like a birth process. Something about love strikes me the most. The process was a peak under the veil, a taste of the love that is beyond words. To see Martha in her own fear was at times difficult—we all face this holding on. Our support was to help her let go and wow, not easy, no matter how "evolved" or what ideas she had about the process. In this way it was human and, again, intimate. Tender, so tender. And something present about what we control and what is beyond our control. Let go, let God.

There is so much I've yet to process about this experience, but I am so appreciative for the gift that it was to me.

In addition to the times when our vigil group met, some of us saw one another in the course of our daily lives, and when we did, inevitably we shared our appreciation and inspiration for having been part of Martha's transition process. I was struck by the fact that while most of the group were either trained therapists, healers, celebrants or seasoned practitioners in mental and spiritual health, every one of them remarked on how extraordinary and unprecedented this experience had been for them. And so the question that came up as I thought about these comments was: Why don't more of us choose this option? Since death is our birthright, why don't more of us, when the time comes, take advantage of, not just the loving services of hospice, but the support of a circle of friends such as Martha created? While my friend Wendy had gathered her immediate family, they were largely unfamiliar with the role that the spiritual, nonmaterial aspect of life plays in influencing our physicality. No matter how the support is structured, however, to stand with someone on the shore and help launch that person into the next phase of their journey can be a profoundly rewarding experience. ❧

SIX

The Secret

If death could be seen
as a beautiful clear lake
refreshing and buoyant,
then when consciousness
moves towards its exit from a body,
there would be that delightful plunge
and it would simply swim away.
—*EMMANUEL'S BOOK*

In the early nineteen eighties, during
my first years of volunteering with the HIV and AIDS
pediatric patients at Harlem Hospital, I got to know

and love a little boy, Sam. Sam had been born at the hospital. and when I got there two and a half years later, he had only spent a short time at home. His family was not able to be involved in his care. Sam was one of the boarder babies, described in the preface. They actually didn't need to be in an acute care hospital, but because in those days there were no other facilities— halfway houses, foster care homes—prepared to take them, they remained at Harlem Hospital. During the first years that it appeared, so little was known about AIDS, fear levels everywhere were acute and widespread. What's more, in those early days of AIDS and HIV, there *were* no medicines or protocols for patients. The very mention of those dreaded acronyms evoked high-level anxiety. The Harlem boarder babies were the subjects of intense medical research as doctors diligently searched for ways to arrest the growth of AIDS.

Sam was the darling of the seventeenth floor. Doctors, nurses, technicians, service staff and volunteers all enjoyed his mischievous sense of humor and loving personality. Sam shared a large room with several other boarder babies, though he clearly was the star. When he was in a good mood, Sam loved to play little tricks pretending, for example, he hadn't drunk his milk when Dr. Simon, as I will call her, the physician who was responsible for the HIV/AIDS pediatric patients, dropped by to see him at lunchtime. He would gaze up at her with his huge, innocent-looking, dark-brown eyes framed by long curling lashes and a head of soft dark curls. When she discovered his milk was actually gone, they would both enjoy a good laugh together.

The hospital's volunteer department procured two or three strollers, and with permission from the physicians, we started taking Sam and his comrades outdoors. A playground with swings and other play equipment was just down the street and a bit farther on was a small park with trees, grass, birds and squirrels. Witnessing the reactions of utter amazement from Sam and the other kids to these wondrous discoveries was deeply touching and rewarding. Sam would point to a squirrel running across the grass or scooting up a tree and then turn to one of us babbling excitedly with his enormous eyes full of questions, waiting for an explanation. Although *squirrel* is a tough word to pronounce correctly, the kids were not shy in attempting it. Birds received similar attention. Some of the picture books upstairs in their room showed birds and various small squirrel-like creatures, but we all recognize what a world of difference exists between looking at a drawing or photograph of an animal and encountering the living, breathing, food-gathering real McCoy just a few feet away.

About six months after the outdoor excursions started, we all noticed that Sam seemed to be regressing. He stopped talking, ate very little, didn't want to go outside, and his bubbly energy was no longer present. One day when I was sitting with him reading a story, Dr. Simon came into the room. She and I had become friendly over time, and she knew I was then studying with the energy healer Barbara Brennan. She asked me, "Do you know what's wrong with him?" I was so taken aback by her question that all I could say was, "No." When we were alone a bit later, she explained that she was concerned with Sam's regressed state. She especially wanted him to be in better shape at this time because in just over a week, she would be leaving to get married and would be away for ten days. She said that every time she went away, Sam's health tended to deteriorate. While I understood her concern, I could offer no insight.

Later that day, as I descended the subway stairs to go home, it came to me all at once and quite clearly—Sam's full story. I realized I *did* in fact know what was going on with Sam. A few days later, on my next trip to the hospital, I sought out Dr. Simon, but she was busy talking with the family of one of the non–boarder baby patients. "When you have a moment," I asked, "may I have a word with you?"

Later when she came into the boarder-baby ward, I was once again reading to Sam. "You wanted to talk to me?"

"Yes," I told her. "After I left here the other day, I realized that I *do* have a possible answer to your question." I was on one side of Sam's bed, and Dr. Simon was on the other side. At this point, Sam tried to push me away. He clearly didn't want me there. "I understand, Sam. This is hard to talk about, but I think it's important that we do," I said. Sam stopped pushing me away but continued to look unhappy about my presence.

Facing Dr. Simon across the bed, I continued, "This is what I know and this is the way that I know it. His entire life, Sam has been doing his best to please all his caregivers here. You, as his chief caregiver, the other doctors, nurses, people who come to take his blood, administer tests, bring him his meals. Everyone comes asking for something, and he has always cheerfully complied." Glancing at Sam, I could see that he had calmed down and was sitting quietly in his bed, though looking somewhat dubious. "Sam is tired," I continued. "He's given all he can give, and now he needs to go home, to truly rest."

Dr. Simon seemed to be taking in my words and trying to fit them into her medical lexicon. As I remember, she said very little, nodding occasionally at my comments with a warm smile focused on Sam.

The next day, Dr. Simon left to get married. I learned later that at the exact moment she and her husband stepped under the chuppah, Sam slipped into a coma and the following day his spirit left his body—he was on his way home.

After she returned to work, Dr. Simon told me that right after our conversation at Sam's bedside, she had put him in a wheelchair and taken him down the hall to her office. "It was like the old days again. He was bubbling over, full of mischief, getting into all the rubber bands and paper clips and other stuff on my desk. We laughed and played just like we'd done in the past. He was his old self, full of life." As she spoke, I could sense her reexperiencing the precious final time the two had spent together, connected by pure love, with no emotional barriers separating them.

Thinking about her story and the power that secrets can wield reminded me of the fun my brothers and cousins and I had as children keeping secrets—upcoming birthday surprises for family or friends—with the feeling that I might burst with excitement before the happy secret could be revealed. These kinds of events were all the more magical because we got to keep a secret. What's more, being motivated by love, they gave us all great joy.

Secrets that are based on fear, on the other hand, can be life draining and destructive. What happened after I gave Dr. Simon my understanding of what was causing Sam's regressed condition seemed to confirm that in Sam's mind and heart my interpretation was essentially correct. Once Sam's "secret" was revealed, he was released from what had been a heavy burden. Pleasing his caregivers—with Dr. Simon as by far the most important caregiver—had been the central focus of Sam's short life. Obviously his relationship to those who cared for him and came to love him had many of the elements of the classic mother/child relationship, that primary bond Simon had never had the opportunity to experience with his own mother. Perhaps the life-filled joy of Sam's final playful session with Dr. Simon—their last time together—was possible because each had let go of expectations that were no longer viable and were causing them both increasing strain to maintain. Thus released, they were able to find unmitigated pleasure in simply being together. ❦

SEVEN

Changing the Story

God said to clarity, *Walk.*
To death, *Help them with discipline.*
To the soul, *Move into the invisible
and take what's there.
Don't sing the sadness anymore.
Call out that you have been given both
the answer and an understanding of the question.*
—RUMI

A couple of years after Sam died, a beautiful little girl was born at Harlem Hospital and took up residence on the seventeenth floor. She was another boarder baby with no family involvement.

When I discovered her in a room by herself, she was no more than ten days old. I remember feeding her a bottle and marveling at her tiny perfect features and large questioning eyes. One of the nurses came into the room while I was there, and we commented on her dainty, shy beauty. She told me they had named her Cecelia. I always made a point of checking on this little one when I arrived at the hospital. One day when I was sitting with her singing her some of my favorite folk songs, Dr. Simon came into the room. "Oh, I see you've got, Cecelia, our little baby with no personality," she said.

"I'm not so sure it's that she doesn't have any personality so much as the fact that she hasn't decided whether or not to stay," I replied. Dr. Simon gave me a questioning look. I went on to explain, "You know when sometimes you're going to a party or a gathering of some kind, and you arrive at the door, look around, and realize you don't know a soul there. There's that moment when you can feel torn between whether to step into the room, make the effort to find your host, introduce yourself to people and see what happens— or submit to the temptation to step back, turn on your heel and head home where you can unwind, settle down cozily by yourself with a good book and a comforting drink. I know *I've* had moments like that. It takes a lot of energy to show up and make your way in a whole new scene without a sponsor or buddy." Dr. Simon didn't comment, but she seemed to be considering my reading of the situation, though I got the feeling she wasn't convinced.

The next time I showed up at the hospital, she came up to me in the hall. "Oh, I want to thank you for what you said last week!" she said.

"What was it that I said last week?" I wondered aloud.

"What you said about Cecelia and her not having decided whether or not to stay," she explained.

Dr. Simon went on to tell me that several days before she and I had previously spoken, Cecelia's vital signs had gone into crisis. A team of doctors and nurses worked on her and managed to stabilize her and bring her back. This is, of course, normal hospital procedure. "Just a few days ago, her vital signs started to go again. I was summoned, but as I stood looking down at our little Cecelia, I thought about your interpretation of what might be going on with her. So I decided not to intervene. I let her go." I could sense that this had been a difficult choice for Dr. Simon, perhaps the first time she had ever made such a choice in her medical career. But what was clear was that she had been able to make it from a place of pure love and, consequently, a heavy weight had been lifted from her heart.

One important thing to remember when considering the concept of "insisting on life" is that it in no way implies *controlling* life. Sometimes true healing entails honoring life enough to let it go. The point is that life—all life, not merely human life—essentially has its own greater wisdom. I suggest that, ultimately, insisting on life means acknowledging and respecting that very fact—the greater wisdom of life. This is at the core of most of the great religions and spiritual traditions. Yet not just in the medical profession, but in so many other ways of our modern life, we humans have become accustomed to thinking that *we* are in charge and can manipulate life to our will. This delusion can take us down some pretty dark and unsavory passages, genetic engineering being just one example. The beauty of Cecelia's story is that Dr. Simon was able to transcend the restrictions of her medical training so that she could recognize and embrace that greater wisdom.

One might say that both Sam's and Cecelia's deaths affirm Walt Whitman's statement from *Leaves of Grass*: "Death is different from what anyone knows, and luckier." 🙢

EIGHT

Is Death the Enemy?

Why do karmic lessons always seem so punishing?

Because you believe they must be so. You perceive yourself as unworthy of kindness, undeserving of the bounty that the planet, your creation, offers you.

You will say, "But Emmanuel, some things cannot be considered as bounty!" I must answer, "Yes, they can." Your task is to utilize everything regardless of its nature, no matter how the world labels it, as a mirror for your own introspection to help you find those pieces of God within you that are hiding. You honor the world completely when you use it for this purpose.

—*EMMANUEL'S BOOK II*

The great challenge we all encounter in the face of death is the reality that there is *absolutely nothing anyone can do to change it.* In recognition of this truth, we often refer to death as "the grim reaper." From high art to modern cartoons, we are accustomed to seeing that hooded figure—face always obscured, holding its menacing scythe—as the symbol of what many would consider the ultimate fear. Over the years, however, working with people on issues surrounding death, I have come to believe that underneath that fear of death is the question of what lies beyond death. Regardless of culture, faith, tradition or absence thereof, it seems that people carry—often unconsciously—an existential fear of being judged and found wanting once they let go of life and pass though the doorway we call death.

In late August of 2001, these reflections coalesced to the extent that I felt compelled to create a new workshop, "Exploring Afterlife Stories and Beliefs," employing, in addition to afterlife tales, several original abstract paintings, live music and a powerful role-play experience. The day after I mentioned this idea to an artist friend, telling him I'd like to use a few of his paintings, I received a call from the program director of a local healing center asking, "Jane, do you have any new workshops?" I told him about my ideas for exploring afterlife issues. "Sounds interesting," he said. We scheduled the new workshop for a date in early November. I pulled together a team of two musicians and my artist friend, and outlined the workshop, explaining the parts they would play.

Ten days later, on September 11, the terrorists' attack on the World Trade Center in New York City hit. A couple of days after that, the director of a different healing center where I had also given workshops called saying, "We have a number of therapists and healers here who are really freaked out. Their clients are in even worse shape. Would you have anything that might be helpful?" I told her about my new workshop.

On September 18, fourteen people went through the first daylong "Exploring Afterlife Stories and Beliefs" experience. One of the exercises we did was to have everyone experience a simulated journey through a human arch "doorway" from life into what might lie beyond death. Each person rotated, playing all the different roles: journeyer, loved ones attending the dying person, the doorway, greeters on the other side of death. The loved ones and the greeters were given different written instruction as to how to relate to the journeyer. The entire exercise was performed in silence with only the sounds of a wooden flute and European harp filling the room. At the conclusion, people sat in a circle and reflected on what they had experienced in the different roles. At the end of the day, people indicated that they felt considerably relieved in a number of ways. Some said they felt more grounded, others less traumatized, still others freer, and generally they claimed to be less confused and fear burdened.

No question, I could sense a palpably different energy in the room at the conclusion of the workshop. What really struck me, however, was that had I not already done the preliminary work of thinking through, designing and preparing this experience, I could never have been able to pull it together and deliver it one week after 9/11. In hindsight, I realized that strong impetus—dating back to early August—to activate my ideas on addressing people's underlying fears behind death seemed to indicate unseen hands assisting the process. In recent years, scientific research has compiled an impressive database of evidence describing these kinds of precognitive experiences. For some scientists, therefore, they are no longer considered merely folklore, but have a respected place in the ever-evolving story of consciousness.

People in everyday life can benefit from pondering all kinds of experiences from different points of view just as those in the "Experiencing Afterlife Stories and Beliefs" workshop did. Sometimes, especially with the elderly, death is a welcome presence. We speak about the angel of death who comes to deliver the person from pain and suffering. In those situations, we may immerse ourselves in mourning the person who has died, while accepting the death. A friend of mine, for example, joyfully described her ninety-seven-year-old, beloved mother's death as "Mom's Graduation into Glory."

When faced with the death of a young person, on the other hand, it's a whole different story. Unleashed, our deeply held sense of injustice can trigger any number of responses to deal with our intense feelings of anger, guilt, outrage and helplessness. Some of us choose to coat those feelings in a thick layer of numbness as a way to protect ourselves from excruciating pain. Others sink into their feelings, whatever they may be, experiencing them fully. Still others engage in vigorous activities, such as providing support for the bereaved family. I suspect that buried underneath this natural urge to help our friends and neighbors, before, during and after the death of a loved one, is often a subconscious longing that's crying out: "Perhaps if I keep busy enough there will be no way for those dreaded feelings of helplessness and rage to take hold."

It was only during my early years as a volunteer with the HIV/AIDS pediatric patients that I began to explore some of the complex issues that surround how people relate to death. This period coincided with my two years of intensive study with the energy healer Barbara Brennan. With Barbara we were learning about the human energy field and how its many different levels influence our thoughts, feelings and behavior, as well as our physiological systems. The two quite different experiences—studying energy with Barbara and hanging out with the HIV/AIDS kids at the hospital—over time opened me to appreciate both life and death from a vastly broader perspective than I had previously known. In the early years of the AIDS crisis, because there were no effective medications available, many people, including infants and young children, died. Yet, never did I witness signs of fear or anxiety as these young children approached death. They seemed to slip away with grace and quiet dignity without any indication of resistance or dread. Gradually, I came to the realization that fear of death is learned behavior, not embedded in our DNA.

As humans, most of us share the belief—an illusion really—that we are in control and have the power to change situations that are not to our liking. When faced with death, this belief shatters like the most precious Ming vase in an earthquake. How to respond? We can, like King Lear, rage at the storm. Or, like so many of our spiritual sages over the centuries have urged us, humbly recognize that both life and death are ultimately beyond our power to control. With this second choice comes a willingness to experience all our feelings, understanding that feelings contain useful information about who we *really* are. Our emotions, especially those that we would rather not acknowledge, when examined compassionately without judgment, can reveal hidden parts of us that may long for healing, reconciliation and acceptance. This inner work often allows us to embrace rather than resist the true reality of death. Death can then be approached not as an "enemy" but more as our trusted mentor. ❧

NINE

The Commander-in-Chief

Here I will stand with my hands empty,
mind empty under the moon. . . .
And if something takes my life,
if a sudden wind sweeps through me,
changing everything,
I will not resist.
I am ready for whatever happens.
—MORGAN FARLEY, "CLEARING"

When her father, Adolfo, was diagnosed with brain cancer that had metastasized from other parts of his body, his daughter, Ana Lia, declared, "It was as though his great love for his family was an umbrella over us, protecting us all." At the time, Adolfo was one month shy of turning ninety-three, so there was no question of trying medical intervention. He accepted that he had entered the final chapter of his life, although at the same time he held the possibility of being cured. The moment she got the news, Ana Lia knew intuitively that her job was to be with her father, the father she had always adored and whose unequivocal love she had experienced in return. This commitment to put her own life on hold, devote her attention to taking care of her father, as well as giving support to her mother, was a courageous one.

Ever since she had separated from her first husband when she was twenty-eight, Ana Lia had felt a definite rejection by her mother, and some of her siblings, as well as her extended family. It was as though they considered her a kind of "black sheep," no longer truly a part of the family. Divorce is not accepted in the Catholic faith, and Ana Lia's family was Catholic with a strong devotion to their faith. Even though she raised her two young sons with loving attention, still she continued to feel the power of her family's nonacceptance. But not her father, his love never wavered. Five years after her divorce, Ana Lia remarried and in time gave birth to two daughters. This marriage has been deeply fulfilling, continuing to grow and strengthen. "But during all those years, I couldn't say how I honestly felt amongst my family of birth because I was always afraid of hurting someone's feelings," Ana Lia confessed.

Her decision to take loving action to manage her father's dying process changed everything. "I found I was no longer afraid about hurting others. It was as though I was experiencing an entirely new order, a new way for me to be in the world with my family." When the five siblings (Ana Lia is the third daughter with two younger brothers) first met with their parents to discuss their father's situation, it became clear that palliative care was indicated. Palliative care is focused on relieving suffering, but doesn't attempt to cure the disease or condition. Ana Lia was the only one who was familiar with this practice, so quite naturally she took the lead. She agreed to stay at her parents' house during the weekdays and organize their household so her father had everything he needed. This would allow her mother, Gladys, to concern herself with being a loving support to her husband of sixty-seven years. Gladys's two other daughters each took Friday and Saturday, her younger son stayed with them on Sunday nights, while her older son took care of all the logistical and financial matters.

Very quickly Ana Lia's relationships to her mother and her siblings were transformed. It was as though the "prodigal" daughter had returned. They all recognized what she was doing and came to appreciate her in an entirely new way. For her part, Ana Lia found that under these circumstances she could say things to her family that she had never been able to say before. "I had the sense that I was steering my family into another dimension," she declared, in a tone of awe and wonder. And her family was experiencing *her* in an entirely new light—as her authentic self, rather than imposing their expectations of someone they thought she "ought" to be.

One month after diagnosis, Adolfo and Gladys asked their priest, who had been coming to the house regularly, to have a ceremony renewing their marriage vows. This event was attended by about forty family members, plus a few close friends. "Receiving communion every day and holding hands in a circle of gratitude with whatever family were present, these were important sacred moments for my father as a way of protecting my mother and the rest of his family," Ana Lia observed.

During this period, when different members of the family gathered around their beloved patriarch, all sorts of stories and secrets came to light. Adolfo especially, who was very truthful and had no inhibitions, shared, without fear or shame, some of his secret escapades from the past. The overarching environment of love was so strong, it dissolved anything and everything in its way.

From 1966 to 1968, Adolfo had been commander-in-chief of the Argentinean Air Force and was well known throughout the country. This was during an Argentinean revolution when a democratic president was overthrown and replaced by a general. Having just returned from a two-year post in Washington, D.C., as Argentinean representative of the three military forces to the Organization of American States, and being a strong believer in democracy, Adolfo did all he could to reverse the political situation in his country and move it toward democracy. His efforts in this direction were unsuccessful, but he did accomplish major improvements to the air force. He replaced old equipment with modern planes *without* resorting to the usual system of bribes. He also established two new flying schools, which still exist today. "Because he had been an air force officer of the highest rank, he was assigned an officer to help us through his dying process. Mainly this involved administrative matters such as his will, honors, the burial ceremony," Ana Lia explained.

When word got out about his cancer, many, many people from all over the country came to see him, and others connected by telephone. Over the course of the six weeks of his final illness, he lovingly received them all. In addition to his many friends of all ages, he spent time with his grandchildren and great-grandchildren. Receiving Holy Communion every day was also an important and powerful source of support for both Adolfo and Gladys, as well as their large family.

During the first weeks of his illness, when visitors came to pay their respects, Adolfo would often entertain them by bursting into song with one of the popular and haunting tangos from the twenties such as "Mano a Mano," roughly translated as "We're Even." This creative expression of lightness of spirit as a way to say farewell came as a big surprise to everyone. Ana Lia admitted, "We certainly didn't expect that." Ana Lia's younger daughter, nineteen-year-old Dulce, recorded her grandfather singing "Mano a Mano," made copies and gave them to everyone. A steady stream of visitors continued to arrive or telephone, which meant that Adolfo was able to experience the equivalent of being present for his own "wake." All these people were able to express their love and gratitude while he was still a living presence, fully conscious and able to receive their tributes.

At one point, Dulce, during one of her visits to be with her grandfather, lay down with him on his bed. She asked simply, "Are you afraid, Tata?" (Adolfo's family nickname) "Afraid of what?" was his reply. Ana Lia commented, "It was as though *he* was taking care of all of *us*." An awesome task given that Adolfo and Gladys, in addition to their five children, had twenty-one grandchildren and thirty great-grandchildren.

One family member, a son-in-law, felt he needed to relinquish his previous role as Adolfo's physician. In this situation, he wanted to be a son not the doctor, so for the most part he stepped aside from his physician role. Palliative care was not part of his medical training and experience. This, of course, is a reflection of the widely held belief that death is a mistake, a failure, some even labeling it a "crime."

"Up until the last day, the process of dying was not painful. This was a huge surprise to me," Ana Lia admitted. One day Adolfo fell to the floor and needed help to rise. "You have to let me go," he said to Gladys. "While he clearly knew he was dying, there was not a hint of fear," Ana Lia said. At this point, the entire family realized they needed to focus only on what was good for Adolfo. A couple of weeks before he died, Adolfo elected to stop eating and taking liquids. Initially upset when he first started refusing liquids, Ana Lia consulted her brother-in-law. He recommended offering small sips of water every half hour. For the final ten days, Adolfo took neither food nor liquids. Right up until the day he died, Gladys slept each night by her husband's side, following his lead, and as she had done through-out their marriage, continuing to be a steady source of support to the very end.

A day came when Ana Lia had a strong intuitive sense that something had changed. "I felt an opening, so I called my family to alert them that I felt Papa was coming to the end of his journey," she said. Then two days later, as they stood around the bed holding hands, in addition to their love and appreciation, the most powerful feeling they shared was one of respect. "Papa died as he had lived—courageous in death as he was in life," Ana Lia said. Throughout his life, his motto had been, "You do what you have to do."

Following the Argentinean custom, after his death, Adolfo's body remained at the house over night. The family lit candles around his bed, arranged him as though he were in sleep. People approached him to say their final good-byes, some touching him as they had in life. The priest celebrated Mass that evening, at-tended by about forty family members and over sixty friends. The following morning the undertakers ar-rived, placed Adolfo's body in a coffin and transferred it to the cemetery. At the cemetery chapel, there was a very simple ceremony with a few prayers and brief eu-logies by the priest and Ana Lia's older brother. "Then we made a procession on foot—family, friends, Papa in his coffin—to the grave site," Ana Lia explained. "When we arrived, we were astonished to see a huge crowd of three or four hundred gathered."

"At the burial, everyone was happy," Ana Lia said. An air force brigadier general spoke, a few more prayers were said and then Adolfo was lowered into his final resting place while an air force bugler played "Taps." What was unusual about this ceremony was the feeling shared among the assembled mourners of love and joy. Later, many people said they left the cemetery that day feeling uplifted. As one person commented, "I've never left a funeral so happy."

One grandson, in an e-mail to his grandmother, aunts, uncles, cousins and parents, wrote in part, "Thank you all, from my heart, what you're doing for Tata. You created a perfect environment for us all to feel comfortable visiting Tata and Mama in the last months. I was always moved entering Tata's room, feeling the perfect temperature, a perfume in the air, all clean and spotless. It demonstrated the phrase 'never better than at home.' It was so comforting knowing that one of you was always there, keeping us informed. Tata died quietly, as my uncle said today, 'Mission accomplished,' thanks to you."

After Adolfo died, Gladys found herself at peace. This she had not expected. She thought she would be in anguish and pain. She kept saying to Ana Lia, "This peace I have is not mine; I wasn't like this. Your father was like this. He left me his peace of mind." There were other indications of ways that Adolfo's spirit continued to uphold and sustain his family. They had a tradition of holding Saturday barbecues at Adolfo and Gladys's house. These happy gatherings had been suspended during Adolfo's illness. The Saturday after his death, however, the family got together for the first barbecue without their beloved Tata. As Ana Lia recalled, "A few days earlier we had had a conversation about how we connected to the other side to be in touch with our loved ones and the different ways those connections manifested." It happened that the day of the barbecue, one of Ana Lia's sisters was sitting at the table holding her baby grandson in her lap. Around her neck was a pouch containing her cell phone and a small electronic device she used to play music. "Suddenly, without warning, my father's voice singing that tango, "Mano a Mano," emerged from her chest. We were so touched and uplifted; it was as though he was assuring us of his continued loving presence."

Two months after Adolfo's death, the family held a ceremony at their parents' house. The priest celebrated Mass, and then, as he had done during the last days of Adolfo's illness, he made room for everyone to express themselves. The principal feeling that afternoon was one of gratitude. Gladys spoke of being grateful for the sixty-seven years she had shared with her husband. Ana Lia, too, spoke of her gratitude. For her, it was her deep appreciation that her relationships with her family had been healed. Clearly the commander-in-chief's spirit was still wielding its influence. ⋘

TEN

Two Brothers

Be patient toward all that is unsolved in your heart
and try to love the questions themselves.
Do not seek the answers that cannot be given you
because you would not be able to live them.
And the point is, to live everything.
Live the questions now.
Perhaps you will then gradually, without noticing it,
live along some distant day into the answers.

—RAINER MARIA RILKE

After almost eight decades of what the younger brother, Dave, described as a "Cain-Abel relationship, a lifelong sibling rivalry," the relationship changed, said Dave, "in the twinkling of an eye and was completely resolved in a few moments."

A lifetime of being taunted fell away one morning when Dave entered his brother Bruce's hospital room to find him "in a state of euphoria." This most uncharacteristic frame of mind came just a few days after Bruce had experienced a terrifying dream/vision while in the ICU recovering from an emergency operation on his spine to keep him from becoming paralyzed. The surgeons were limited in what they could do, however, because of the stage-four prostate cancer that had spread to his spine. In his ICU dream/vision, Bruce described being in a straitjacket in a large room surrounded by all the people he had always loved. They were telling him that they had never loved him. He was horrified. Then, in the dream, he had a revelation. He realized he was a complete hypocrite, not the person he had always pretended to be. In part of the dream, Bruce was doing battle with evil creatures—the nurses, doctors, others—all trying to destroy him.

"He had always thought he was doing good things in his life until he suddenly came to see he really wasn't," Dave explained. "I was stunned. In a way, it was so close to the truth. He kept telling me, 'It was so *physical!* My own flesh and blood! They're all working against me, doing evil things to me.' He wanted me to write it all down." Dave (and other family members) listened to this nightmare description and wondered whether it might have been, at least partly, triggered by the painkiller/anesthetic. Later, Dave likened Bruce's nightmarish dream/vision to the first part of Dante's Inferno. "It was as though he had suddenly become clairvoyant and could see what other people were thinking. I had bad-mouthed him for years, behind his back. And I was full of remorse about that," Dave admitted.

In contrast, he describes Bruce's unexpected subsequent transformation as the result of his "having *seen*. He had seen that life is bigger than death, that even where he lay dying, there was so much life all around him. The ladybugs on his hospital window, the nurses, family—he *knew*, he said, that life triumphs over death. 'And that includes Dad!'"

This was a family with a long history of controlling behavior by male family members, where being "right" held high value. Both Bruce and Dave had fought countless battles with their father, who only at the very end of *his* life was able to release the fierce grip he had always maintained on his role as the authority figure. With Bruce and Dave at his bedside, at last their father was able—somewhat awkwardly but simply—to express his love to his sons. Now, Dave realized, Bruce had walked through that same doorway. "Suddenly all defenses were down, we could speak to each other as never before. All animosity was gone, and there was nothing but love flowing between us. It was like absolution." Instead of half dreading visits with his older brother, "Now I want to be with him as much as I can before he dies. I think it may turn into a very good time," Dave wrote to a friend right after that experience. "He was in a really good place, tapping into his inner joy, accepting the whole thing."

"I remember we laughed about some of Dad's silly made-up expressions. What was so powerful was not necessarily their intrinsic humor as the fact that we could appreciate them *together*—there was nothing standing between us any longer. Instinctively, we recognized that was *definitely* worth celebrating. I only wish we'd had *more* good times together at the end."

As Dave looked back over Bruce's many life accomplishments, he reflected, "It was as though he'd put on spiritual seven league boots and was striding in them. He was learning fast and trying to tell us as fast as he learned. We were there, like people trying to rescue precious things from a burning house. What I think he was trying to tell us is that life is greater than death, that joy is deeper than sorrow." 🌾

ELEVEN

The Snows of December

Even when you are dead
You are still alive.
You do not cease to exist at death.
That is only an illusion.
You go through the doorway of death alive
and there is no altering of the consciousness.
It is not a strange land you go to
but a land of living reality
where the growth process is a continuation.

—EMMANUAL'S BOOK

In the dream there is no illness, no paralysis. I walk through the storm, filtered streetlight reflecting the swirling snows. The last year has taken a toll, I feel a need to rest. Moving past houses, softly lit through the windows, deepens the sense of alone.

I sense them inside, sitting quietly beneath the lamp, book in hand or speaking softly at the table, using the moment so casually. They are filled with the illusion of time, of tomorrows, of plans and hopes.

Yet I am alone in an entirely new way. Although I have never been this way before, I feel it is where I am meant to be, where I have always been. A new and somewhat frightening perspective fills me; it is a glimpse of where time and distance end.

The wind swirls the flakes even faster now, into a random dance that happens once, just once. I revel in its ephemeralness. I pull the drawstring tighter across my neck, bend my head down, rub my hands together and move on. Now, with each step I feel closer, warmer, lighter. The brightness inside seems to shine through each pore. Oddly, I notice my hands no longer feel the cold. The pain in my chest is gone, no cancer has me, my legs feel strong and alive. I could walk forever in this state, I am certain.

Now I notice the snow has stopped falling, the storm has calmed. A moon as I have never seen before hangs above the open field, illuminating the way. I turn to look behind and am surprised to see no footprints in the sparkling snow, snow that reflects an image, an image of a life left early. The snows of December came early.

Ahead I see a welcome space before me, one empty yet full, silent yet full of sound, beautiful, inviting sound. I am nearly home at last. I see now I had never left.

Bernie wrote this piece nine months before he died. He titled it "When the Snows of December Came Early." At the time of writing, after having been a paraplegic for almost a year and then seven months later diagnosed with cancer, he didn't know whether he would live or die. His wife, Lola, discovered this piece among his papers after he died. "Bernie was an awakened being, always searching for God. He had been a spiritual seeker all his life. On our first date, we talked about God. This was amazing to me as I would never have imagined this long-haired hippie being so spiritual. He was my guru, a wonderful, wonderful person," she declared.

"We loved to go camping. The weekend that Bernie fell in our pool and broke his back, spontaneously we decided to go camping in the Alleghenies, just the two of us. The weather was beautiful. We hiked, kayaked and fished, cooked over a campfire, sat by the water's edge and gazed at the sunset, thoroughly enjoying our surroundings and one another. When we left on Sunday morning, we looked at one another and said, 'This has been our best camping trip ever,'" Lola remembered. "At one point Bernie said to me, 'I'm not going to live to be an old man.' My response was, 'I don't want to hear this,'" Lola said. In the course of his life, Bernie repeated that same statement a number of times. "We used to argue about it, with me always saying he was full of baloney."

Everything changed late that afternoon when they returned home and invited family over for a swim and cookout. Bernie slipped and fell into their pool, emerging with help from his nurse daughter, saying he couldn't feel his legs. At the hospital, they discovered he had broken his back and sustained a severe spinal cord injury. Subsequent surgery, during which he almost died, was followed by severe pain. Bernie's doctors never told Lola that he had died during the operation and was revived only with great difficulty. Bernie, however, from his hospital bed, described *his* experience during surgery.

First he said there were no words in the human language to convey what he had seen: He told his daughter and son-in-law that he went to a healing garden. There were other "souls" there, but he couldn't see them. He was in a carved-out tree stump full of golden sawdust. The garden was terraced, and everything was made of light—colors vivid beyond description. There were healing guides there who spoke to him, using telepathy as their means of communication. He was totally at peace and didn't want to leave. A guide came to him and said he had to go back. Bernie was reluctant, but was given the tree stump and other herbs and plants to take back with him for healing.

After two months of rehab, Bernie finally came home in a wheelchair. The rehab people told Lola that Bernie was the hardest-working patient they had ever seen and that they had never expected him to leave alive. Some months later, he developed an infection, a kidney stone, and then came news of his stage-four prostate cancer. The urologist had estimated he had two months to live. "When chemo didn't work, we tried lots of alternative treatments," Lola said. "I did reiki on him; he went on the hallelujah raw food diet; I took him to a holistic practitioner." Bernie's spirits rebounded to the extent that he and Lola were able to go camping, even though he was still wheelchair-bound.

At this point, while Bernie did not want to die, he wasn't *afraid* of death. Shortly before he died, he told one of his daughters, "I'm going somewhere I've never been, and I'm never coming back." Lola sensed, however, that even though *he* was prepared to die, he had trouble with the idea of leaving his family. They had depended on him for so much, he worried about how they would get on without him. To make matters more difficult, *they* didn't want him to leave. "That made it hard at the end," Lola confessed. "I realized he was getting ready to depart, but the girls weren't able to accept his dying and were hanging onto him energetically."

During this period, Lola met and got to know a psychic practitioner who told her about a healing process she facilitated for people. Over a number of weeks, Lola and she became close friends. When she heard about Bernie's situation, she asked Lola whether she would like to participate in a special healing process. Lola readily accepted the invitation. The process involved the healer psychically inviting three angels to visit Bernie and Lola, who could ask the angels for three wishes if they chose. Because the healer had so many requests for these visits, Lola and Bernie had to wait their turn for several weeks. "By the time it was finally scheduled, I realized that Bernie had entered a stage of actively dying," Lola said. "The angels came and stayed with him until the night of our celebration after his death. In time, my three wishes all came true."

About two month after Bernie's death, one of his granddaughters, eleven-year-old Kimberly, reported having had this dream. "I was sitting in the red chair in the bedroom. Papa had just died, and I could see him smiling. He was sitting up, but his body was still lying in the bed. He seemed very happy. Granma and Grampa Morris, Uncle Tom and Aunt Laura were with him. I knew who they were because I have seen pictures of them even though I never met them. Everything was happening up near the ceiling. There were three other people there I didn't know. They walked Papa out the front door." Lola asked Kimberly what these three people looked like. She replied, "They had wings."

Two weeks before he died, Bernie told Lola that he had just seen his dead mother walk by. Meanwhile, Lola was feeling really stressed, not knowing whether she could continue to take care of him full-time. In his final days, Bernie told Lola that he was receiving visits from a number of deceased souls who were of prime importance in his life—his mother, father, sister, Jesus. One day during this period, Lola said to her husband, "I don't know how I can go on without you after you leave." Even though his speech had become weak and garbled, he responded to her very clearly, "I am always here." "It gave me such chills," Lola said.

After his death, one of Bernie's daughters reported having had this experience. "I was lying down as an attempt to sleep. I don't know how much time had passed, then suddenly I felt like I was with Dad where he was, and I couldn't see him but I knew I was with him. Then I began to hear voices, or thoughts maybe. It was a 'traffic' of thoughts that knew people's lives, from beginning to end, and they were choosing what life they wanted to experience. Again, there were no visuals, but the 'thoughts' were flashing lives, from birth to childhood, then into adulthood. They were happy to choose that path and take on that life. Suddenly I felt an overwhelming, burning pain, and I can only believe the pain I was experiencing was from Dad's perspective. Like what he felt knowing he was going to leave us. I became aware that I was not asleep and that I was crying for his loss."

"Since Bernie died, I've had many signs from him, I know he's with me, especially when I write in my journal," Lola said. Over the years, to help her better understand how to deal with her life, Lola occasionally visited a medium. During one of these sessions not long after Bernie's death, the medium told her that he had been given a choice. He could choose to move on spiritually or stay connected to his family and wait for Lola. "He's waiting for me to die so we can go on together," she said. "I talk to him every night."

While Lola has been able to accept the death of her dearly beloved husband and is at peace with how their relationship has evolved, she feels quite differently about one of her parents. "My father's death had been peaceful. I was able to spend time with him before he died, and I was complete, at peace in my relationship to him. It was different, however, with my mother. When she was getting ready to die, I was so caught up in caring for Bernie, I was unable to spend as much time with Mom, as I had with Dad." As a result, it's been much harder for Lola to deal with making peace with her mom's death.

Lola admits, "I miss Bernie every moment. Each day is one day closer to being with him. I live each day fully, always with love, compassion and in giving as much as I can. That's what I've learned from him. Love fully, give of yourself and live like each day is your last. As his sister said before she died, eat more ice cream and climb more mountains. And that we did! We never had fancy vacations. We just enjoyed the simplicity of nature and spending time together and with our family."

This story illustrates that when people are open to exploring spirituality beyond what their upbringing or culture may embrace, they can have rich and rewarding experiences. When this exploration involves their relationships to life and death, the experience can be profoundly transforming. What's more, this perspective can spread beyond those actively engaged in exploring expanded realities. Eleven-year-old granddaughter Kimberly knew nothing of her grandparents' angel visitation. Yet she was quite clear as she described her dream of having seen three people she didn't know—with wings—escorting her grandfather out the front door. Bernie had been a spiritual seeker all his life. Lola was attracted to him for that reason and continues to follow in his footsteps. Even though some may find this story a bit fanciful, it affirms the quote from Emmanuel that introduces this chapter, the last sentence of which is, "It is not a strange land you go to but a land of living reality where the growth process is a continuation." ≪

TWELVE

Community

May you live all the days of your life.
—JONATHAN SWIFT

This is the story of how a family dealt with the sudden, accidental death of a greatly beloved twenty-year-old member, Greg. Unexpectedly plunged into overwhelming despair, the family immediately reached out to one another and gathered around Greg's parents to offer loving support. In the process, the family found it was able to engage with death as part of life. Step-by-step events unfolded that led them from that initial utter darkness eventually to a place of life-sustaining light.

It's worth noting that the manner in which this particular family dealt with Greg's death and its aftermath rested on a long tradition of creating do-it-yourself projects. In their perspective on the world, handcrafted was regularly the preferred choice over store-bought items. They were raised on finding nontraditional ways to honor and commemorate all manner of important—and not-so-important—occasions. The operative motivation generally was to create an authentic, joy-filled event crafted by the shared participation of everyone involved.

Shortly after Greg's death, a seemingly unsolvable dilemma arose when a fast decision had to be made as to what to do with Greg's body. His mother, Anne, opted for cremation, while his father, Fred, was adamant that Greg should not be cremated but buried. "But where?" Anne agonized.

Neither parent was part of a church community. Anne struggled with this new sort of grief. "I don't want him buried in some anonymous cemetery where we have no connection and no one will ever want to go." Yet Anne recognized that Fred was suffering, too, and knew she needed to respect his needs. How to resolve this core issue? She saw only a huge unbridge-able chasm.

Immediately after Greg's death and for the next several days, neighbors took on the task of protecting the family from being overwhelmed by guests. They also fielded funeral home questions, adopted the role of newspaper liaisons, and aided with everything from obit writing to securing Greg's death certificate. While Anne was struggling with the dilemma of where to bury Greg, other friends were stepping up to handle a whole range of critical tasks behind the scenes. They re-searched spaces to hold the memorial and carried out all the arrangements once a place and date were cho-sen. One neighbor took on the task of finding beds in the neighborhood for arriving family. Her husband be-came airport pickup steward, faithfully meeting and de-livering family members to their generous hosts.

Much later, Anne acknowledged that she never could have done what she did at the memorial and afterward if she hadn't had so much amazing support. Together, a whole community of neighbors and friends took on the "heavy lifting," as Anne called it, thereby allowing her and Fred to find quiet times for reflection. They were able to think through how they wanted the ceremony to be so as to capture Greg's true spirit and share it with everyone. ❦

THIRTEEN

Setting an Intention

Today we are sad and grieving.
Someone who was with us is no longer here.
So we let the tears flow
and give ourselves fully to weeping.
But in our mourning let us not despair . . .
for anything we lose
comes around in another form.
As every dead tree
becomes soil for new life,
each season dies
to become the next season;
as each day goes down to become night,
and night dies to dawn, and dawn to day.
Nothing perishes.

—AUTHOR UNKNOWN

Even though Greg's parents had different ideas about how to handle their son's bodily remains, there was no question they both equally cherished him and were equally devastated by his death. When faced with the death of a loved one, these different choices are not uncommon. Some folks will go to great lengths to visit the body of the deceased, hosting and/or attending wakes and "viewing" sessions. Others prefer to connect to and communicate with their loved one's nonmaterial essence—what is often called their spirit or soul. Still others deem it important to engage in both these practices. I suspect our universal love of sharing stories about the deceased person we love may be an effort to reconnect on both of these planes of reality.

As Anne and Fred were struggling with the dilemma of how and where to dispose of Greg's body, a good friend, Bert, offered to set aside a few acres of his several-hundred-acre rural property for Greg's burial place. With this unexpected and generous gesture, a workable resolution began to take form. For the family, it was as though a doorway had appeared in what had previously been a solid wall.

From different parts of the United States, Anne's three siblings began to arrive with their families. They each cared deeply for Greg and naturally were badly shaken by his death. Within minutes of their arrival, spontaneously, they gathered in a neighbor's backyard for an impromptu family softball game. One team, no score keeping, everyone got on base, including Greg's almost three-year-old youngest cousin and his grandma. "That baseball game was so important," Harry, Anne's younger brother, remembered much later. "To be honest, I wasn't in great shape, barely holding it together. Just being able to hang out with everyone, taking part in a very ordinary physical activity helped ground me, kept me from flying apart."

In those first days after Greg's death, it was as though everyone—both family and friends—was experiencing every waking moment through a giant magnifying lens that exaggerated the size and intensity of even the smallest event. This is, no doubt, how organic systems in shock respond—nothing is ordinary or taken for granted, everything is writ large, underlined and in bold. The assembled cast of characters that was drawn to honor and celebrate Greg's all-too-brief life was rich, colorful, included a broad range of talent and, above all, abundant love. Everything that subsequently transpired stemmed from that base.

As plans for a memorial service were developing, with neighbors taking care of the many details, more than one friend came to the house predicting: "There's going to be a big crowd there!" Among the numerous behind-the-scenes tasks to be tackled was arranging the many flowers that had been sent to the house and bringing pitchers of juice, bowls of fruit and platters of homemade cookies to make the town hall feel welcoming for the Sunday afternoon service. Later, people reported they were struck by the sense of cheerfulness they encountered when they entered. They felt it signaled that this was going to be an important celebration.

One of the hallmarks of true community—interconnectedness—is that people tend to let go of ego and personal needs. Intuitively, they find ways to support a greater intelligence, thereby accomplishing what often can look like miracles. I am reminded of physicist David Bohm's comment, "The most important thing going forward is to break the boundaries between people, so we can operate as a single intelligence. This is the natural state of the human world, separation without separateness."

The day before the memorial, about twenty people—family and a few close friends—drove to Bert's property to choose Greg's burial spot and prepare his grave site. Harry, a building contractor, was thoroughly qualified to direct this task. His older brother, Bob, a landscape architect, was an apt assistant. Bert's property was equipped with backhoe and all the tools needed to do the job. Under Harry and Bob's direction and with Bert's blessing, this was how they managed a family affair. Once again, the physical labor provided a healthy outlet for feelings of helplessness that accompany intense grief, especially after the unexpected death of a young person.

Many months later, Anne's three siblings provided vivid recollections of their afternoon of grave digging. Anne's sister, Carol, remembered, "Watching Harry operate the backhoe that afternoon was like watching an artist. He had such patience with others! He invited everyone who wanted to, to take a turn at the controls. Operating a backhoe is really hard; it's very three-dimensional. While others were digging, the rest of us were clearing away small trees with brush cutters and machetes. It was good to have something constructive to do, lots of physical work. Everybody wanted to participate. It felt great to attack the brush and just whack it down.

"I remember thinking that this is something people all over the world and throughout time have known how to do, but most of us have never experienced dealing with death at this level," Carol said. "I was struck by the rawness of it all—the land, our emotions. Yet the whole process was organic, real, pure, undiluted. It was not concealed, not hidden, not manicured, not dressed up: It was just the way Greg himself was. I remember thinking, 'What an amazing family I have! I'm so lucky!'"

Harry remembered, "You know how Bob is always telling me how to do things? Well, there was none of that going on. He was right there with me all the way. And having Carol there was *so* important! Just knowing she was there meant everything."

"It seemed like the natural thing to do." Bob recalled. "After all, we're doers." It wasn't the first time he'd helped dig a grave. "It felt like it was the last gift we could offer to Anne and Fred and the rest of the family as a way to honor Greg." Bob was the first one to get up on the backhoe with Harry. "He wanted me up there to set an example so others would want to try their hand. I've operated a backhoe before, but I'm no expert. Harry is a true natural master. It was frustrating work because the ground was so hard, progress was slow. On the other hand, the fact that it took so long wasn't a bad thing because it meant everyone who wanted to had a turn on the backhoe. Harry and I got down in the hole near the end to finish off the digging with shovels. As I remember, someone gave us a hand up when we had it squared away as best we could."

At day's end, back at Anne and Fred's house, the grave diggers gathered for dinner—a delicious meal provided by loving friends. Even though they had toiled mightily and were physically spent, their labors had been a pivotal contribution to expressing their love for Greg, as well as for releasing some of their pent-up feelings of loss.

As separate conversations bounced around the table, it felt more like a holiday than a wake. Everyone was acutely aware they had participated in a pivotal, even transformative, life experience. Yet there was no way any of them could have spoken of this on that evening. Some experiences can affect us so profoundly that it may take months, even years, to be able to share them with others. Instead, the family talk around the table that evening focused on topics they could easily handle. "So how do you like living in Montana?" "How's the tourist season this summer on Cape Cod?" "I hear you're going to be studying in England next semester." Incidental, easy-to-handle conversations.

Everyone was relaxing after dinner when, without warning, Greg's four young female cousins burst onto the scene, each sporting an astonishing moustache— quite distinct in color and shape. The room exploded with laughter. The kids pranced around, enjoying their effect on the disarmed adults. "When the kids came out wearing those moustaches," Bob recalled, "it broke the sadness; it gave us a new way to vent our bottled-up feelings."

In such an environment, fear of death has no currency. ❧

FOURTEEN

A Celebration

Nature doesn't distain what lives only for a day. It pours the whole of itself into each moment. We don't value the lily less for not being made of flint and built to last. Life's bounty is in its flow, later is too late. Where is the song when it's being sung? The dance when it's being danced? It's only we humans who want to own the future too . . . The death of a child has no more meaning than the death of armies, nations. Was the child happy when he lived? That is the proper question.

—TOM STOPPARD,
THE COAST OF UTOPIA: A TRILOGY

On Sunday afternoon, over five hundred people made their way to Greg's memorial service, filling the town hall to overflowing. As is not uncommon at secular memorials, upon entering, people were greeted by a continuous loop of Greg pictures—infancy to the present—playing on a large screen at the back of the stage, accompanied by some of Greg's favorite music, all prepared by friends and neighbors. The long tables on both sides of the room, laden with flowers, fruit, juices and cookies, provided a cheerful and, for some, a surprising element.

In the course of the service, both Fred and Anne shared stories of Greg's special, playful nature, quirkiness and wisdom, apparent from a very early age. Other family members, Greg's high school history teacher and friends added their loving stories—some hilarious, some deeply poignant—of Greg's unique way of engaging with the world. Halfway through the program, the entire assemblage was invited to share their favorite Greg story with one another. People were encouraged to turn to folks near them, folks they might not know, to tell and hear a Greg story. People reported the room came alive with a buzz of heartfelt remembering. This opportunity for everyone to participate greatly enhanced an environment of loving intention that was palpably building.

Two of Greg's college friends had a different approach to storytelling. They had put together a DVD showing glimpses into Greg's extracurricular college life. Some of the people present that afternoon reported that the lively antics captured on the video were evidence of young people enjoying one another and vying for ways to demonstrate their creativity and aliveness. Since Greg was always up for adventure, it's not surprising his friends shared that quality.

After a few more rollicking stories, the mood shifted as small strips of paper and pens were distributed to the assembled mourners. This time, they were invited to pen a wish for Greg, whatever might come to mind. A gentle quiet, spawned by loving intention, grew until it filled the room as everyone welcomed another opportunity for active participation. Greg's young cousins collected these precious miniature scrolls in baskets, and eventually they found their way to Anne and Fred's house.

The following April, the family celebrated what would have been Greg's twenty-first birthday. Gathered in their garden, they set afire the five hundred loving wishes and burned them as a way to transform all that love and share it with the universe.

Back at the town hall, at the end of the ceremony, as people were preparing to leave, a man came to the front of the room and announced, "I have a two-hour program on our community radio station every Sunday evening. Tonight I will be devoting the entire show to Greg's favorite songs. I hope you'll listen in." Not only Greg's family but also many friends tuned in to hear Greg's favorites that evening. Some may have been surprised to hear the voices of family members commenting on the selections and telling more Greg stories between the numbers. The station being close to Fred and Anne's house, one by one they wandered up the street for the opportunity to share their love for Greg through still more storytelling. ⫸

FIFTEEN

The Burial

There are sorrows enough for the whole world's end
There are no guarantees but the grave
But lives that we live and the times that we spend
Are treasures too precious to save.
—BOB FRANKE, "THANKSGIVING EVE"

Early Monday morning, eight vehicles carrying family and a few close friends caravanned to Bert's property for the burial. The first stop was the funeral home to collect Greg in his coffin and place it in Bert's large van. Once there, family members took turns carrying the coffin down the meandering path to the spot where the empty grave awaited. The rest of the group followed behind, carrying bunches of flowers.

Three sturdy, wooden four-by-fours had been placed across the hole. When everyone had gathered, eight people lifted the coffin one last time and placed it on top of these spanners. Next, Bert and Bob slipped two lengths of a strong hemp rope under the casket. Some of the pallbearers stood on either side of the grave holding tight to their end of the rope, while others rolled aside the spanners. Deftly managing the ropes, those holding the coffin slowly lowered it into the grave with no conversation or hint of confusion.

A longtime family friend, Karen, had prepared a Bob Franke song. Her normally strong, clear, voice sounded uncharacteristically fragile as she sang the bitter-sweet yet lilting melody.

> *It's so easy to dream of the days gone by*
> *It's a hard thing to think of the times to come*
> *But the grace to accept every moment as a gift*
> *Is a gift that is given to some.*

Tentatively the group joined in the chorus after each of three verses:

> *There are sorrows enough for the whole world's end*
> *There are no guarantees but the grave*

But lives that we live and the times that we spend
Are treasures too precious to save.

After the last chorus, there was a moment of silence as each person tended to his or her own emotional needs. Then Fred invited people to speak their thoughts and prayers. For some, it was a moment beyond words. Those who carried flowers tossed them into the grave on top of the coffin, adding quiet words of love and farewell.

Up until that moment, with the notable exception of the absence of any professionals, this simple ceremony had consisted of what most people experience around the grave site of a loved one. What came next, however, took the group into an entirely different realm, instantly connecting everyone to Greg's special world. Without words, as though in response to a prearranged hidden signal, appeared rubber bands of all sizes and colors. Family members—parents and children alike—proceeded to shoot these, slingshot fashion, into the grave. This somewhat unorthodox burial ritual had its origins during the time of a family Christmas gathering. Harry explained, "We were all gathered at Dad's house, and I grabbed a handful of rubber bands, turned to Greg and said, 'Let's go hunt some little girls.' Together we snuck all through the house like bandits.

When we heard giggles coming from my old room, I kicked in the door and we shot the four girls straight on. They responded with howls of rage, picked up the spent ammunition and took off after us. Thus began the first of the great rubber-band wars."

The rubber bands were not the only unusual items to go into the grave. One of Greg's cousins tossed in a green Lifesaver. Of course, there was a story attached to it, and of course, it had to do with Greg. The summer before Greg died, the entire family, while on vacation together, was gathered around a small pond, looking for goldfish. In her excitement, the youngest member, not yet two, tumbled into the pond, which was well over her head. Instantly, Greg plunged in after her and fished her out, soggy and sputtering, but unharmed. From that moment onward, he was known as the Lifesaver. "OK," he declared, "If I'm going to be a Lifesaver, then I want to be a green Lifesaver." At the grave, the green Lifesaver was followed by a barrage of Greg's favorite foods—a banana, a can of tuna, a Pop-Tart, a bag of chips and a Mars bar. Carol remembered, "At this point, as I looked around our circle, I noticed the mood was considerably less somber."

Bob and Harry picked up two shovels and started to shovel in the dirt. One by one, thirty people took turns with the shovels so that each could have a hand in the ancient ritual of grave filling. Eventually, the hole was filled with a good mound rising above grade to allow for settling.

As the finale to the ceremony, they planted a small maple tree that a friend had given the family. The young eagerly scampered off to refill their empty water bottles from a nearby pond to soak the thirsty transplant.

Job done, there was a shared reluctance to leave. ❦

SIXTEEN

An Insistence on Life

This we have now, it is not imagination.
This is not grief or joy.
Not a judging state, or an elation, or sadness.
Those come and go.
This is the presence that doesn't.
—RUMI

Like so many others, Anne's friend, Karen, confessed that she was devastated when she heard about Greg's death. She didn't know what to expect at Anne and Fred's place, but nevertheless, she was frantic to get there. The first thing she noticed was the overwhelming support coming from the community. "I was shocked at how emotionally uptight I was during the entire trip. Arriving at the house surprised me with its light. It wasn't dark; it was filled with *life*. There was an *insistence* on that. It was then I realized I had a basic fear about people dying."

"The experience was simply one surprise after another," Karen continued. "We were there making it all happen. It was *so filled* with life. Anne and the others, they invited people in." Karen found that the inclusion experiences at the memorial ceremony were where she, like so many others, found solace. "Usually at funerals, everyone is separate," she said. "The storytelling and the wishes connected people. And it was overwhelming in its power. It was so expansive and the embellishments of humor were so comforting! It all said, 'We're going to be OK!' It was an opening, the opposite of a closing."

At the burial, Karen felt that walking the distance from their arrival point to the grave site was like being in another country, another time. And she was glad for the space, hopeful that she could ready herself. "I was filled with fear seeing the hole gouged in the earth," she said. "It said to me, 'This is the worst thing that can happen to you.' I was amazed at everyone's strength and fortitude. Nobody said, 'I don't want to do this!' Everybody helped and created a sense of ceremony. There was a solemn moment, then people were throwing things into the grave, like we'd made a turn that said, 'Let's get on with it!'"

Over the years, Karen had been with the family in a variety of situations, but this was new to her, as of course it was to all of them. "God bless Bob and Harry," she'd thought at the time, "for finding the strength, doing what they know how to do. It's as though they, too, were each saying, 'I can do this. I'm going to continue to be in relationship with Greg. And then when it came to singing the song, I said to myself, '*Now* I can do something!' It was an incredible gift to be able to sing that song."

"I'm still trying to figure it out. Anne is the first person in my life who's said, through her actions, 'It's OK to die!'"

∘ ∘ ∘

Several years after Greg's death, I was asked to officiate at the funeral and burial of a woman in her mid-fifties. While she had previously been diagnosed with cancer, her death came unexpectedly prematurely to her loving family and friends. As I discussed with her husband the details of how he wanted to structure the funeral service and burial taking place immediately afterward, I asked whether he might want to have those at the burial throw dirt into the grave on top of the casket as a way for everyone to participate in the ceremony. He didn't feel comfortable with that idea, so as an alternative, I said, "What about collecting a bunch of beautiful autumn leaves and offering them to the mourners to toss into the grave as loving tokens?" He liked that idea, perhaps because his wife had been a professional landscape and garden designer. In addition to her family, gardens and nature were her two great passions. When we came to the place in the burial ceremony for the leaf tossing, a large shallow basket appeared, and because it was a breezy afternoon, it was carefully covered with a colorful cloth. The thirty mourners, one by one, each chose a few leaves while I explained their role in this simple ritual and encouraged them, if they wanted, to offer a silent, loving prayer.

A couple of days later, the husband called to thank me for officiating at the ceremony. He especially wanted me to know how grateful he was for the leaf-tossing ritual. The day before the funeral, he had taken a couple of family members with him, and they'd gone to a nearby park in search of colorful leaves. "I found that time so very helpful," he said. "There we were in nature, and I felt truly close to Andrea, the world that she so loved. It was an unexpectedly healing time for me—earth centered, quiet, peaceful, with nothing but love to contemplate." ⟨⟨⟨

SEVENTEEN

This Mysterious River

As We Move Deeper
into this mysterious river, I pray
that our work stay real; that we do
not turn everything we touch into us;
that we help each other listen more
deeply than we have ever listened;
that we baptize each other
with what we find there;
that we heal each other's
blindnesses by pouring love like
water on each other's eyes;
and that waking in this way,
we make the unseen breath of God

visible, the way that wind can only
lift a tree that has grown in the open.
—MARK NEPO

What can we learn from these differ-
ent stories? How might they help us in adjusting our
relationship to both life and death? For each person,
the answers to these kinds of questions may be different
because we each carry our *own* unique story with us.
Our individual life experiences, especially those during
our early years, tend to set patterns that can stay with
us our entire lives. For instance, Gretchen, a child of
war, had been terrified of death ever since she could remember. At age four, when World War II began, she
had several extremely frightening dreams: always
falling into a dark abyss and dying. This fear of death
remained with her for much of her life. For instance,
she was unable to be present when someone was dying
or visit a funeral home or cemetery. Only as a mature
adult was she finally able to throw off these overwhelming feelings of terror concerning death.

In January of 1994, a few days after Gretchen and
her husband had arrived in Mexico for their usual winter stay, she had a telephone call from her elderly

mother in Germany. Gretchen could tell from her voice that all was not well. When she asked her mother if she wanted her to come, the reply was a most uncharacteristic and barely audible, "Yes." At once Gretchen realized she needed to go to her mother. But she was also very worried if she might not be strong enough to face her mother's possible death.

With her husband's blessing, she was able to make all the arrangements without any obstacles, so that the following day she was in Germany. She found her mother very weak, close to death, but as she greeted her, Gretchen discovered there was nothing but a powerful feeling of unconditional love between them. Completely gone were her lifelong fears concerning death. She sat with her mother, holding her hand, totally filled with feelings of love and peace. Six hours later, her mother died, leaving Gretchen completely at peace, still immersed in feelings of love and gratitude. This experience of releasing her previous fear of death has continued to sustain Gretchen so that some years later when her husband was dying, she could once again engage in the same process she had experienced previously with her mother: a complete absence of any resistance or fear, sustained by their overriding mutual love. Gretchen might describe this life-changing shift as the result of her having been able to move beyond ego to a place where fear has no currency—only her sense of unconditional love. True transformation is just that—a one-way passage that takes one into an expanded reality.

As an addendum to this story, recently Gretchen told me she had decided to enroll in a program that would train her to be a hospice volunteer. When she completes this course, she is looking forward to devoting herself to being with the dying and easing their passage through the doorway from what we call life to its partner, death.

In the earlier tales, we see brief examples of different people who unexpectedly were also able to release their fears concerning death. The specific circumstances differ, but the resultant feelings of elation, of being released from a heavy burden, are similar. In most of those cases cited, I knew none of the particulars of what had been healed. What was abundantly clear, however, was the extent to which each person felt genuine relief. As the fellow in the federal correctional complex blurted out that morning after his day-long workshop, "Death and Rebirth," "I feel so much lighter!" Initially during that workshop, we had focused on helping each man let go of his old, inauthentic self, the self that had led to his being convicted of a federal offense. We had then moved on to have each participant ask, "Who am I *really*?" In these situations, being able to embrace a new self—changing the story—

can frequently produce powerful feelings of lightness and well-being.

With Alice ("The Missing Piece"), her feeling was not fear of death but rather a kind of pebble-in-her-shoe or thorn-in-her-side gnawing feeling that wouldn't allow her to relax. She found herself unable to accept her own profound healing from cancer when her beloved husband, having followed the very same Native American healing protocols, succumbed to his similar disease. Alice's deep sense of basic "fairness" simply wouldn't allow for what seemed like life playing favorites. It wasn't until several years had passed and Alice was in a workshop exploring her own relationship to death that she came to realize in a flash of insight that she had been missing a vital piece of the puzzle. Once she held that piece—the missing information—she could slip it into place, and the picture at last was complete and made perfect sense.

"Tackling the Great Mystery" brings up the challenging question as to whether and to what extent our feelings can influence physical outcomes. Of course, there are so many varied and subtle factors that make up a life, it's impossible to understand them all with any degree of certainty. Reflecting on both Gary's and John's stories may not produce answers or a credible theory. They do invite us, however, if we're willing to consider how our *relationships* to what is—in Gary's and John's cases, cancer—can affect our experience. Denying, resisting or fighting a new reality can be hugely stressful and exhausting. Accepting and engaging with a changed reality can also be a lot of work, but it has the advantage of being focused on love and, therefore, more likely to supply life-enhancing support. It's another reminder of how everything and everyone is both interconnected and interdependent

The overriding motivation in both Wendy ("Embracing Life, Death and Beyond") and Martha's ("Standing on the Shore") situations is one of acceptance. Wendy didn't merely "accept" the terminal nature of her cancer, she actively engaged in and celebrated every aspect of this final chapter of her life journey. What's more, the fact that she could devote so much joyful attention to planning and carrying out her "last act" turned out to be highly contagious. At her funeral, it was clear the extent to which the entire community felt joyfully and gratefully uplifted by both her actions and joyful attitude. Martha, too, was able to create a similar environment of joy-filled gratitude from the group she had called together to support her during *her* final chapter. Perhaps others may be inspired to follow a similar path when the time comes. Certainly, the rewards far outdistance the effort.

We have all had experiences of feeling impelled to keep a secret. Happy secrets can reap rewarding surprises. Sometimes, however, we may feel the need to keep a secret when fear is the motive. "I'm afraid she'll be upset if I tell her." "I'm afraid he won't let me if I tell him." Sam at Harlem Hospital was withholding what was going on with him from Dr. Simon, his chief caregiver, out of his great love for her—the chief substitute mother-figure in his life. This created a heavy burden on his big heart, draining him of his vital life force. Once the secret was revealed—Sam is dying—nothing stood between them, allowing both his energy to return, and Dr. Simon to cease her efforts to initiate "curative" protocols. One could say the "game" had changed radically. Now Dr. Simon's only responsibility was simply to enjoy this very special, mischievous soul on his own terms, as he completed this final portion of his brief life journey. I dare say, both Sam and Dr. Simon carry warm and grateful memories of their last time together.

Cecelia's life journey ("Changing the Story") was considerably briefer, but here again, Dr. Simon was able to expand her medical horizons to include and accept the decision of this precious infant to make her departure. I think one of the lessons found in so many of these tales is the obvious benefit to caregivers and loved ones when they come to recognize the need to relinquish their role as "the controller." Modern science and medicine have developed extraordinary protocols for extending life. The ultimate power to control life and death, however, still rests with the dying. Or should I say the living? This basic issue of where lies the true life/death power switch is one we humans have great difficulty with. As a species, relatively few have evolved beyond the illusion of a need to control life. What is clear is that when the energy of power/control is coupled with fear, the results can be catastrophic. When power/control is hitched up with the energy of love, on the other hand, we begin to catch a glimpse into the untold possibilities of the creative force—life.

This reality was certainly operational during the commander-in-chief's final weeks. The overriding feeling both family and friends experienced during that period was one of love. As Ana Lia said of her father, "his great love for his family was an umbrella over us, protecting us all." This allowed everyone to express their own brand of love in their own special way, so that—as in many of the other stories—everyone felt gratefully interconnected. Throughout it all, the commander-in-chief, as he had during his long and distinguished life, was fearlessly leading the way.

In the tale of the "Two Brothers," only after Bruce and Dave had ceased their lifelong competition, were they able to truly connect. And the shift occurred, as Dave says, "in the twinkling of an eye." Their fierce struggle to win—prove to one another and the world that one was right, good and true—simply evaporated into thin air. Simultaneously, they came to recognize the folly of competing when it was infinitely more rewarding to simply enjoy one another without resorting to suspicious distrust. It was as though the rules of their old game no longer applied. They had moved onto a new playing field with quite different customs and conditions that allowed for—nay, required—entirely different behavior.

With "The Snows of December," we have the element of curiosity as a crucial motivator. Bernie's lifelong search exploring different spiritual traditions was fueled by his fearless curiosity. This drive, being sourced from love, formed the basis of Bernie and Lola's unusually close marriage. The mystic's assertion that Bernie had been given a choice after he died and took the option to wait for his beloved Lola substantially benefits both partners. Some may be skeptical of this assertion, but it makes it considerably easier for Lola to accept Bernie's death and continue to live her life. As she herself states, "What I've learned from him is love fully, give of yourself and live like each day is your last."

The saga of how Anne and Fred and their family handled Greg's sudden shocking death is yet another example of the mysterious ways that interconnectedness and interdependence can fortify and strengthen families even in the most devastating circumstances. No one involved will ever forget those excruciatingly painful early moments and hours after hearing of Greg's totally unexpected, violent death. But by the same token, none will ever forget the mysterious process that unfolded, allowing everyone—family and friends alike—to make choices and take actions that truly expressed their abiding love for Greg and for one another. Once again, the only force more powerful than death turns out to be the power of Life. And, as previously stated, the energy fueling the power of life is love.

Very recently, my dear friend Emily quite unexpectedly died. It was the day before Thanksgiving when the phone rang. One of Emily's closest, longtime friends announced quietly, "She just died. They removed her breathing tube about half an hour ago and she left." I had visited Emily in the hospital two days before and had spoken with this same friend along with a couple of other close friends of Emily's who were spending many of their waking hours at her bedside, as a team of loving presence and support. Before my hospital visit, I had been aware that because of breathing difficulties, she had been sedated and a breathing tube inserted. Over a week before, Emily had entered the hospital for a biopsy procedure. For several months she had been plagued by a number of troubling symptoms, but her doctors had been unable to discover the cause.

The biopsy was an attempt to solve her medical mystery. While I was of course concerned about my friend, the thought that she was in mortal danger had not occurred to me.

I hung up the phone and sat in my desk chair trying to make sense of this stunning news. Without realizing it, emotionally I was being thrown back to my four-year-old self struggling to make sense of my father's statement to my brothers and me in our living room the day after Christmas, "I have very bad news. Mummy has died." My older brother burst into tears at once, my two-year-old younger brother, with his huge blue eyes, just looked from face to face uncomprehendingly. I, too, didn't understand what had happened or what it meant to die, but I did recognize that whatever it was, it was *very* bad because not only my brother but my father was crying. I managed to force a few tears. Back on that long-ago fateful day, my central and ever-mounting feeling had been one of confusion. Now, so many decades later, there I was experiencing that same confounding feeling of bewilderment, coupled with the growing sensation that I had been abandoned. The four-year-old's subconscious lament returned with a vengeance, "You never told me you weren't coming back!"

Fifteen years of giving workshops to help people change their relationship to death from fear and resentment to one of loving acceptance counted for naught. Emotionally, I was right back where I had started at age four—foundering and confused. On the surface, I managed to function as usual, fulfilling responsibilities, engaging with others. Internally, however, I found myself lost in the midst of what felt like a combination of dense fog and an impenetrable jungle on a moonless night.

Three weeks after Emily died, came more shocking news—the massacre at Sandy Hook Elementary School in Newtown, Connecticut. Twenty first graders and five adults were shot down by a twenty-year-old assassin, who then took his own life. The entire nation came to attention around this unthinkable tragedy. People everywhere gathered for impromptu prayer vigils, sending love to the deceased and to that entire shattered community.

Three days after Newtown, at the reception following Emily's funeral, when people were encouraged to offer informal reflections and remembrances, uncharacteristically, I had nothing to offer. The fog-cloaked impenetrable jungle still had me in its grip. Three days after that, I attended a prayer vigil and meditation devoted to the Newtown community. What I experienced that evening cannot be judged in terms of ordinary reality. Not uncommonly with spiritual experiences, it occurred outside both time and space. While sitting in meditation with a group of about twenty others, all at once, this thought dropped fully formed into my consciousness, "*That's* why Emily left when she did! She was called away to help prepare for the Sandy Hook kids when they arrived." Suddenly it all made perfect sense. With that, my fog of confusion simply vanished, and I emerged into the sunlight.

Emily had for many years been the director of the hit TV children's program *Sesame Street*, with six Emmys and other prestigious awards to her name. There was no one on the planet more attuned to the magic of young children—their dreams, hopes, fears, curiosity and innate creativity. Who better to help those first graders get through what must have been a terror-filled doorway from their abruptly terminated lives into what lay beyond? For the first time in a month, it was as though I were back in my own body, feeling grateful and profoundly humble. Having been given this magnificent and what seemed to me authentic rendering of Emily's "story," I felt restored to a place where I could once again truly celebrate death as the inalienable partner to life. ❦

ACKNOWLEDGMENTS ⋘

Over the course of several years, this book has evolved through a number of versions until it finally came together in its present form. This is not uncommon in storytelling. As new information is revealed and new levels of awareness unfold, we often adjust our stories to include expanded or fresh meanings.

First and foremost, I am profoundly grateful to all those who provided the stories used in *An Insistence*, including those who were part of Martha's prayer vigil in chapter five, "Standing on the Shore." Earlier versions of chapter four, "Embracing Life, Death and Beyond," and chapter six, "The Secret," were previously published in not-for-profit newsletters. I also want to thank Susie Wilde and Marjorie Lipari for their fine and careful editorial contributions, Susan Moore for her copyediting and Kate Mueller for her proofreading. I am grateful to Nomi Nassim for his skilled research in helping to track down the copyright holders for the authors of the quotations used in chapter headings. Another vital source of support has been Julia Hill Gignoux of Freedom Hill Design, who has been invaluable with her sensitive and imaginative design, as well as offering suggestions on other production issues. Alicia Evans, my publicist, has been and continues to be an important ongoing source of support for *An Insistence*.

Words are one thing but they can be greatly enhanced by a simple visual image. I am so very grateful to my good friend Elsie Trask Wheeler for allowing me to use her photograph for the cover and throughout *An Insistence*. Her telling and often mysterious bird photos grace numerous walls throughout the land. I am honored to be able to share this one with you.

In addition to these dedicated folk are many others who have listened patiently to me over the years as I struggled to find my way along the path. As every storyteller well knows, without a listener, we are nothing.

- Are you afraid of death? If so, how do you deal with this feeling?

- How do you handle the "unfairness" of death?

- What, in your experience, are some consequences of denial of death?

- What can be the consequences of accepting the dying process into one's own or a loved one's life?

- Can you recall a "tiny moment" when a portal of self-awareness unexpectedly opened revealing a new relationship to both life and death?

- Do you or do you not believe there is life after death? What is the origin of your belief?

- What is your response to the Native American expression: "Today is a good day to die"?

- What does it mean to you to live a good life?

- Is there one story in this book that you particularly identify with? If so, why?

- How do you make the "unseen" visible in your life?

- What do you suppose this life is about for you?

Grateful acknowledgment is made to these publishers and writers:

Preface: Josh Billings, American humorist, 1818–1885;

Chater One: *Emmanuel's Book*, Some Friends of Emmanuel, New York, © 1985, p. 56, permission requested;

Chapter Two: *Emmanuel's Book*, Some Friends of Emmanuel, New York, © 1985, p. 169, permission requested;

Chapter Three: *The Essential Rumi*, translations by Coleman Barks, Harper Collins, New York, © 2004, p. 30, used with permission;

Chapter Four: Marcus Aurelius Antoninus, 121 AD–180 AD, Roman Emperor, A.D. 161–180;

Chapter Five: Henry Jackson van Dyke, American poet, 1852–1933, "Standing on the Shore";

Chapter Six: *Emmanuel's Book*, Some Friends of Emmanuel, New York, © 1985, p. 170, permission requested;

Chapter Seven: *The Essential Rumi*, translations by Coleman Barks, Harper Collins, New York, © 2004. excerpt from "An Understanding of the Question", p. 297, used with permission;

Chapter Eight: Excerpt from *Emmanuel's Book II: The Choice for Love* by Pat Rodegast, copyright © 1989 by Pat Rodegast and Judith Stanton. From on page 71. Used by permission of Bantam Books, an imprint of The Random House Publishing Group, a division of Random House LLC. All rights reserved.

Chapter Nine: Morgan Farley, poet, excerpt from "Clearing," permission requested;

Chapter Ten: Rainer Maria Rilke, Bohemian-Austrian poet and novelist, 1875–1926;

Chapter Eleven: *Emmanuel's Book*, Some Friends of Emmanuel, New York, © 1985, p. 169, permission requested;

Chapter Twelve: Jonathan Swift, 1667–1745, Anglo-Irish satirist;

Chapter Thirteen: author unknown;

Chapter Fourteen: Tom Stoppard, *The Coast of Utopia, A Trilogy,* Grove Press, New York, © 2007 by Tom Stoppard, permission requested;

Chapter Fifteen: Bob Franke, American singer/songwriter, excerpt from "Thanksgiving Eve," used with permission;

Chapter Sixteen: *Rumi*, translations by Coleman Barks, Harper Collins, New York, © 2004, excerpt from "This We Have Now", p. 261, used with permission;

Chapter Seventeen: Mark Nepo, American poet, permission requested.

Made in the USA
Middletown, DE
07 June 2020